This is a book I have prayed wou
with everything in it. I didn't. How
ment that a holistic and biblical
include both search and harvest st
ism and discipleship, church plant
of these are essential elements in reaching the nations for King Jesus.
To neglect even one is to do serious damage to the task of world missions. This book is long overdue. I welcome its arrival. I pray for its
implementation.

— DANIEL L. AKIN, PhD
President, Southeastern Baptist Theological Seminary

North American missions had no more than gotten off the ground
when missiologist Rufus Anderson visited the fields and made an all-
important observation. He concluded that, if missionaries were sud-
denly to be withdrawn, schools, clinics and similar institutions would
most likely continue on. The institution that would suffer most
would be the church! Why? For lack of adequate leadership.

Both missions and missiology have undergone a sea change since
then. But one characteristic persists to this present hour: *imbalance!*
Some missionaries engage in "hit and run" evangelism. Others are
intent on eliminating poverty and transforming society. Both—and
much else—at the expense of raising up responsible, New Testament
churches.

Providentially, the Lord of the Church has been prompting concerned missiologists to research and write with a view to correcting
the imbalances—each from a somewhat different though comple-
mentary perspective. Dr. Sills' *Reaching and Teaching* represents one
of those efforts, and a most worthy one. All mission-minded believers should read this book. All missionaries should put its principles
into practice. All instructors should read and teach it. This to the
establishment and maturation of Christian churches all around the
world.

— DAVID J. HESSELGRAVE, PhD
Professor Emeritus of Mission,
Trinity Evangelical Divinity School

Is the missionary to reach the unreached and move on to other
unreached peoples? Or is the missionary also to teach and disciple
those reached? Dr. David Sills deals with all the issues swirling
around this fascinating topic. His credentials as an experienced missionary and a fully qualified scholar give him authenticity to grapple
with this important issue. I highly recommend this book for its
breadth and depth of biblical, theological, and pragmatic insights and
its highly readable style.

— DAVID M. HOWARD
Former President, Latin America Mission.

David Sills is a brilliant missiologist, a faithful teacher, and a missionary of long experience. In this book he puts all that on the line to clarify some of the most urgent issues in Great Commission ministries today. This book must be read by any serious person committed to the Great Commission.

—R. ALBERT MOHLER JR., PhD
President, The Southern Baptist Theological Seminary

David Sills knows what it means to be a missionary, taking the gospel to those who have never heard the transforming message of King Jesus. He also knows what it means to be a seminary professor, training the pastors who will build up the churches of the next generation. In this provocative book, Sills calls on Great Commission Christians to rejoin the training of pastors with the global proclamation of the gospel. Even those who do not agree with all of Sills' recommendations will benefit by engaging with the questions he raises. This book is gospel-fiery, heart-empathetic, and mission-practical. It is provocative in the best sense of the word.

—RUSSELL D. MOORE
Dean, School of Theology,
The Southern Baptist Theological Seminary

Reaching and Teaching is a welcome exposé of what sorely lacks in much mission that emanates from the 21st Century Western church, including, sadly, its mission agencies and seminaries. No serious-minded missionary of significant tenure in cross-cultural ministry can read the first forty pages without acknowledging the frequent and sometimes ruinous mistakes often made by rookie missionaries. Brave that gentle rebuke and you will find the remainder of the pages to provide hard-won wisdom and insight that only comes from one that has learned hard lessons the hard way. Dr. Sills has earned that right to be heard. I encourage missionaries and those who train them to listen well and learn.

—DAVID SITTON
President, To Every Tribe Ministries

Reaching every people group with the gospel is the task of the church. In *Reaching and Teaching*, Sills provides helpful guidance about the pace of the discipleship and training process of indigenous church leaders. With passion, he calls on missionaries, agencies, and the church to make theological training a cornerstone in the work of reaching the nations for Christ.

—ED STETZER
President, LifeWay Research

REACHING
AND
TEACHING

A CALL TO GREAT COMMISSION OBEDIENCE

M. DAVID SILLS

MOODY PUBLISHERS
CHICAGO

Editor: Dana Wilkerson
Interior Design: Ragont Design
Cover Design: Brand Navigation, LLC
Cover Image(s): SIM (Serving In Mission)

Library of Congress Cataloging-in-Publication Data

Sills, Michael David, 1957-
  Reaching and teaching : a call to Great Commission obedience / M. David Sills.
    p. cm.
  Includes bibliographical references (p.   ) and index.
  ISBN 978-0-8024-5029-6
  1. Indigenous church administration. 2. Great Commission (Bible)
  3. Missions—Theory. I. Title.
  BV2082.I5S56 2010
  266'.023—dc22

                                                                2009046988

We hope you enjoy this book from Moody Publishers. Our goal is to provide high quality, thought-provoking books and products that connect truth to your real needs and challenges. For more information on other books and products written and produced from a biblical perspective, go to www.moodypublishers.com or write to:

Moody Publishers
820 N. LaSalle Boulevard
Chicago, IL 60610

1 3 5 7 9 10 8 6 4 2

Printed in the United States of America

To
Abraham Michael Sills
My first grandchild
May the blessing promised to your namesake
in Genesis 12:1–3 be yours also.
And like him, may the families, clans, peoples,
and nations of the world
be blessed through you.
Papi

A NOTE TO
THE READER

Missionaries are my heroes, godly men and women working as hard as anyone at home, but doing so in other languages, suffering homesickness, culture shock, and unstable governments, leaving the comforts of home to live amidst persecution, tropical diseases, and violence, compelled by the love of Christ and His missionary call. Missionaries follow the Lord's calling on their lives, faithfully employing their unique gifts in the places where He calls them to serve. They increasingly must devise creative access to the countries closing their doors to missionaries every year, balancing ethical concerns with gospel need. I am thankful for mission agencies and missionaries who are aggressively engaging unreached, unengaged, and uncontacted people groups that are often in the most gospel-hostile parts of the world. I am equally thankful for mission agencies and missionaries continuing to disciple, teach, and minister in other fields. Almost everyone agrees that both reaching and teaching are biblical and essential aspects of Christian missions, and to some extent, that each is under way around the world in a host of diverse ministries. But there is much that is not being done and the result is tragic.

While I want to encourage those reaching the unreached to continue that vital work, I also want to exhort us all to do more than just reach—much more. Jesus commissioned us to teach everything He has commanded. A biblically balanced missiology includes searching, reaching, harvesting, church planting, discipling, and teaching. The Lord Jesus, the missionary Paul, and biblical commands exhort us to reach and win the lost, disciple them, and teach teachers among them.

What is the biblical balance in the missionary task? Turn the page, and let's begin.

—M. David Sills

CONTENTS

FOREWORD

Is there mission beyond evangelism? Jesus certainly said so. Great Commission Line 3: *"Teaching them to observe all that I have commanded you."* That's how disciples are formed. And disciples (not converts) are what He told us to make. The apostle Paul certainly thought so. His first priority was to preach the gospel and plant churches. But then he worked tirelessly to make sure they grew in depth and maturity. He re-visited them. He wrote letters to them. He answered their questions and challenged their mistakes. He agonized in prayer for them. In fact he may well have spent more time in mission beyond evangelism than in evangelism itself. He spent nearly three years in Ephesus teaching that church the whole counsel of God from the Scriptures so that it became a source of evangelistic expansion to the whole region (Acts 19–20).

And alongside Paul there was a whole network of other church leaders whose *primary* missional vocation was in mission beyond evangelism. Think, for example, of:

- *Apollos* (Acts 18:24–28). His work was **teaching** the church. He was already converted and well-educated (in Africa), but he received even better biblical instruction from Priscilla and Aquila (in Asia) and then he went and used his gifts for strengthening the church through Christ-centred biblical teaching (in Europe—how's that for a missionary career?).

- *Timothy* (1Timothy 2:2). His work included **training** others to be able to preach the truth of the Scriptures, as he himself had learned from Paul. Mentoring and training multiplies those who can handle the Bible well and teach it to others.

- *Tertius* Who? He was the one whose job was **writing** down the great letter of Paul to the Romans (Romans 16:22). Writing was a special skill, and people with something to say needed the help of good writers. Peter needed Silas for that job too and commended him as a faithful brother for doing it (1 Peter 5:12).

Teaching, training, writing—all of it happening in the New Testament church. And all of it equally necessary for the growth and health of the church. And all of it a vital part of the *mission* of the church. Paul would not tolerate the idea that he or Apollos were any more important than each other. "What, after all, is Apollos? And what is Paul? Only servants . . . I planted the seed, Apollos watered it, but God made it grow" (1 Corinthians 3:5–6).

The importance of this "Apollos factor" in Christian mission was recognized by John Stott, in the ministries he founded, which I am privileged to serve, in the Langham Partnership International (known as John Stott Ministries in the USA), which trains pastors in biblical preaching, encourages evangelical writers for their own contexts, and supports theological education in the majority world. This is "church growth" mission—growth in depth, not just in numbers.

David Sills' passionate plea in this book is addressed primarily to the missions community in the USA, but it is long overdue and needs to be heard by missionary-minded churches worldwide—including those who see the USA itself as among the "mission fields" of a world in which biblical mission is (as it always was) from everywhere to everywhere.

> —Christopher J. H. Wright
> International Director, Langham Partnership
> International (John Stott Ministries, USA)
> Author, *The Mission of God: Unlocking the Bible's Grand Narrative*

INTRODUCTION

In recent years, mission agencies and missionaries have increasingly shifted away from teaching and discipleship toward an emphasis on evangelism and church planting—some to the exclusion of any other field activity. While evangelism and church planting are essential components of a missions program, deep discipleship, pastoral preparation, and leadership training must be priorities as well. Jesus explicitly called the church to make disciples of the nations and to teach them to observe all He commanded us (Matthew 28:18–20). However, it seems that today many well-intentioned missionaries believe their task is merely to evangelize and then group willing participants into new "churches."

As AD 2000 approached, mission agency administrators and field missionaries sought to reach the world by every means possible as quickly as possible. An awareness of unreached people groups (UPGs) grew out of this time period and dominated missions efforts in the last quarter of the twentieth century. This awareness spurred agencies and missionaries on to identify and reach these groups. The accompanying sense of urgency shifted the missiological community away from time-proven strategies to more creative methods, hoping for rapid expansion of Christianity. These trendy, creative methods included new approaches to church planting, eschatologically driven missiology, and, all too often, a reductionistic interpretation of the Great Commission. The result of the application of these method-ologies is such that once a targeted UPG hears the gospel, many mis-sionaries move on and turn their attention to the next UPG. Unfortunately, these well-intentioned efforts to reach the unreached result in an inadequate approach to missions.

This understanding that the most pressing need is simply to reach UPGs and then continue to the next one results in a strategy to reach, preach to, and leave as many people groups as possible and as fast as possible. Discipleship, leadership training, and pastoral prepara-tion are unfortunately relegated to a lower level of ministry that is not really considered missions. Some missionaries even consider any effort expended in such areas an impediment that slows down the "most important work" and is therefore an enemy of that which is essential.

This new understanding of the task of international missions is so common today that many consider it to be normative. Since the prevalence of this methodology has been growing for well over a decade, we are now seeing its consequences and ramifications. The most frequent consequence is that churches left in the wake of such efforts either fall apart rapidly and disappear or degenerate into dys-functional gatherings with unbiblical doctrine and practice. As a result, the new believers are often victims of aberrant doctrine, heresy, cult outreach, or nominal Christianity for the rest of their lives. The church the missionaries leave behind is very often anemic at best and a syncretistic aberration at worst. The second unfortunate consequence is that proven, traditional missiological methods, strate-gies, and philosophies are now considered to be "old-school," out of touch, and overly complex paradigms that hinder rapid, exponential growth. However, rather than viewing theological education, pastoral preparation, leadership training, and in-depth discipleship as lesser forms of missionary activity, we must return to the biblical understanding of missions that incorporates them as primary and necessary ways of fulfilling the Great Commission.

Born out of my own research and burden to faithfully serve the call of Christ in the Great Commission, it is my prayer that this book will clarify the task of international missions. Of course, each of the subjects treated in the following chapters deserve more attention than I can devote in a single book. I am not attempting a thorough and exhaustive missiological treatment of each of these crucial issues; rather, my aim is to highlight modern trends that have arisen in recent decades and to suggest correctives that are based on such treatments provided elsewhere. Through an integration of the Scriptures, missiological research, and case studies, this book will help missionaries, pastors, and students wrestle with the biblical foundations and the holistic task of missions. The Great Commission is not just about evangelism or church planting. Jesus said to *make disciples* of all the ethnic groups of the world and to do that *by teaching them to observe all that He commanded* us (Matthew 28:19–20).

1

TEACHING THEM: THE GREAT OMISSION OF THE GREAT COMMISSION

Evangelical missionaries and mission agencies are eager to finish the task of world missions. Having recognized the need to reach all the people groups of the world, recent decades have found missionary efforts increasingly focused on the goal of completing that task as quickly as possible. However, in the midst of their focused and fervent efforts, many are now realizing the need to define the task or to reconsider the total task of international missions. Slogans such as "The world in this generation!" rally the faithful and call out the called, but to do what? The need for specific task definition must still be addressed. As missionaries have joined the race to reach the unreached people groups of the world as quickly as possible, they have strategized to increase speed. The need for speed has influenced missionary efforts so much that many traditional missions tasks have been jettisoned in order to enable it. Indeed, in recent years it seems that increasing the speed has itself become the task. Evangelical missions organizations have been busy operating both traditional and creative ministries all around the world. Yet some missionaries have been looking over their shoulders at the wake of their efforts and are seeing a church that they barely recognize.

We received the Great Commission two thousand years ago. How are we doing? Over one-third of the world—more than two billion people—has never heard the gospel. Approximately one-half of the world's people groups remain unreached. Among those we reached in past decades, new generations are questioning the shallow and often syncretistic versions of Christianity that their parents believe. Still, some would say that we have finished our work among the "reached" because they have churches. Others would see that much work remains.

It matters what teachers teach and what believers believe. In an age where media and movies promote pluralism and many churches have embraced inclusivism, most evangelicals still believe in the exclusivity of the gospel. On the other hand, adherents of pluralism teach that every religion has value in and of itself. They hold that sincere followers of other religions will be saved through their respective religions. Missionaries with this perspective believe that the essential goal of their ministry is liberation, freedom, and basic morality for their hearers. Adherents of inclusivism teach that since Jesus knew that everyone would not have a chance to hear the gospel, He included all religions in His work. The goal of missionaries with this perspective is often simply to help people find Jesus in their own religious systems. However, if we adopt pluralism or inclusivism, we cut the root and nerve of missions.

Exclusivism teaches that there is no other Savior than Jesus Christ alone and that you must be born again. Moreover, we believe that, apart from being born again by grace through faith in Christ, people are separated from God and will spend eternity in hell. Missionaries with this perspective seek to proclaim the gospel message and fulfill the Great Commission in obedience to Christ, to rescue the perishing, and, above all, to bring glory to God. Sadly, not all Christians in the world are convinced of this truth.

THE SCOPE

In medical schools, there are some students preparing to be research scientists to find a cure for cancer and others who are planning to be family physicians. If we compare the work of missions to the medical field, we would say that the work of a missionary is more like that of a family physician than that of a research scientist. The research scientist may find the cure he seeks and declare his work to be done. However, a family physician will have many diverse duties, such as caring for patients during flu season, setting broken arms, and experiencing the joy of delivering babies. His work will continue changing to meet pressing needs all of his life. Mission work, also, is always ongoing, changing, and developing.

In the 1960s, some began to consider the work of the Great Commission to be complete. A brief study of any global missions map showed that there was a church in every geopolitical entity called a country—or nation. Since Jesus commissioned the church to make disciples of all nations, the work must surely have been completed. Yet in Matthew 28:19, Jesus actually said, "Go therefore and make disciples of *panta ta ethne*," not every geopolitical country. The word *ethne* means "ethnic group" or "people group." Based on this, Ralph Winter spoke at the 1974 Lausanne Conference for World Evangelization and highlighted the Great Commission challenge of reaching not only the countries of the world, but more specifically the ethnolinguistic groups that populate it.

Even though the task of reaching all these groups is not yet complete, a new challenge is emerging. Today's challenge is to go beyond merely recognizing the legitimacy of people group thinking to understanding what our task should be among the people groups. Even as Dr. Winter clarified a part of the Great Commission so that we would not be merely thinking in terms of geopolitical nations, we would do well to remember *what* Jesus sent us to the ethnolinguistic groups to do. Jesus did not say, "Go therefore and get decisions from people, then gather them into groups called churches," although both of these steps are essential parts of the Great Commission. He in fact said, "Go therefore and make disciples of all nations, baptizing them in the name of the Father and of the Son and of the Holy Spirit, teaching them to observe all that I have commanded you" (Matthew 28:19–20). It is the command to teach that I want us to consider as we begin to understand the task of international missions.

THE NEED

As God allows me to travel the world, preaching, teaching, and leading mission teams, I have seen a common thread. This thread is the biblical illiteracy of many national brothers and the de-emphasis of theological education and thorough preparation on the part of mission entities. The danger of this is compounded as it coincides with an alarming new reality in global Christianity.

In a new emphasis (or de-emphasis), some major agencies have so focused on church planting and evangelism that they have neglected the need for theological education, pastoral training, and leadership development. Some have reasoned that in order to fulfill the Great Commission, we must pour our efforts and resources into evangelism and church planting. Some even believe that Jesus cannot return until we reach every people group—and that He will return immediately after we do.

When Ralph Winter began to point out the long overdue need for people group orientation, his organization estimated the world's people groups to number 24,000. They have since revised that number to 27,000 as some of the unreached groups have received more study and are now considered to be two or more distinct groups. Other missiologists consider the total number of the world's people groups to be around 11,000. Virtually every person or agency calculates the number of people groups in the world differently.[1]

Another point for consideration is what Jesus meant in Matthew 24:14 about preaching the gospel to all as a testimony. "And this gospel of the kingdom will be proclaimed throughout the whole world as a testimony to all nations, and then the end will come." Many missionaries have preached the gospel through interpreters or without understanding the cultural adjustments that are necessary to communicate the gospel clearly. Additionally, some people hear the gospel for years before they truly hear it! So what does it mean to have preached it to a people as a testimony? Is it merely pulling into a village, preaching John 3:16 through an interpreter, and driving away?

What if we reach all the people groups that we consider to be unreached and yet He delays His return for fifty years, or five hundred years, or five thousand years? What will happen to all of the people who have heard the gospel, raised their hand to pray a prayer, and then watched the dust of the missionary's vehicle as he sped away to the next people group? Who will teach new believers? Will the churches confused with syncretism, the Mormons, the Jehovah's Witnesses, or the Muslims be the ones who take them in and teach them?

Students who feel called to an international theological education ministry often express concern about the few opportunities they find to teach pastors on the mission field. Some agencies have greatly reduced the available openings for theological education in order to invest more human and financial resources in reaching unreached people groups. These agencies certainly care about those who need training, but the push has been to place their missionaries among the unreached. Subsequently, traditional mission fields are being left in the hands of the nationals regardless of whether they have the biblical training to sustain the furtherance of the gospel.

One problem with this approach is failure to fulfill Jesus' Great Commission instruction, "teaching them to obey." Some say that they will fulfill this by encouraging new believers to obey all that Jesus commanded. However, they will not be staying around to do the teaching. They further state that the new believers have a Bible and the same Holy Spirit we have; He will guide them into all truth. Yet syncretism, aberrant doctrine, and blatant heresy remain in many churches around the world.

THE NEED ILLUSTRATED

I recently met a number of Nigerian students pleading for help in their seminary. Many of them needed classes in order to finish their preparation, graduate, and serve in churches, but there was no one to teach the required courses. This plea for help is all the more concerning because the church in Nigeria is suffering much confusion. There are thousands of churches in Nigeria—Baptist, Methodist, Presbyterian, Pentecostal, Assemblies of God, and AIC churches (African Independent Churches or African Initiated Churches). Many Nigerian churches preach a "name it and claim it," "power in your mouth," "health and wealth," and "seed money miracle" gospel message. Many are so far from the truth that the truth is very hard to find. In a country that is struggling with poverty and crime, many have turned the church into a miracle cult. Since I am Southern Baptist, I painfully noticed many Baptist churches in Nigeria that have adopted this philosophy of ministry.

Southern Baptists entered Nigeria in 1851. When the Southern Baptist Convention (SBC) began in 1845, it formed the Foreign Mission Board (FMB) and the Domestic Mission Board to engage in missions. The FMB chose China and Nigeria as two of their earliest mission fields, and Nigeria is the oldest continuous mission field for Southern Baptists. It was once regarded as the "White Man's Graveyard," and the advance Baptists gained there was purchased at great cost. So why, after so many years of work, do many of the Nigerian churches have such aberrant theology and practice? I began to wonder what had gone wrong. Is there a lesson to learn in the history of the Southern Baptist work in Nigeria?

Today there are some 8,500 churches and 4,000 pastors in Nigeria.[2] Animism still reigns in the hearts of most believers. Some churches use juju to bring crowds to their meetings. One of the professors from the Nigerian Baptist Theological Seminary reported that some large churches sacrifice cows and bury them in juju ceremonies in order to bring forth power to attract and sway the crowds in their church services. Even many of my seminary students there were not convinced that juju is demonic. They believed that it could be a neutral, ambivalent force to be manipulated for good or ill by the initiated. These were graduate-level students of the oldest theological seminary on the African continent, founded in 1898.

THE VOID THAT I continually see is an indigenously-led discipling process that is reproducing among Africans. I am speaking of the simple but profound process of knowing how to access Scripture and ask the right questions and model the process well enough so others can "catch" it and take it home. Possibly one of the greatest teaching needs is a discipling process that can be given away—one that really fits African lifestyle and learning styles—a process that will allow Africans to excel at making disciples. I am passionately committed to the pursuit of that discovery.

—STAN WAFLER
Missionary, Northwest Uganda

As they have for decades, many of the students still view Jesus primarily as the honored ancestor. The belief in ancestral spirits is saturated throughout all aspects of their traditional culture. This "honored ancestor" idea prevents them from seeing Jesus biblically as the reigning, interceding, and soon-coming King. Nigerian Baptists have had SBC missionaries among them for more than 150 years —not counting all the other denominations and their efforts. Yet they still struggle with these concepts. Having a Bible and the Holy Spirit is not adequate without someone teaching them. It is obvious that they still need to be trained to interpret the Word of God accurately.

Additionally, their cultural worldview is that the ancestors hold and have an impact upon time. In the timeline perspective of this view, people living today stand still, and the only time with which we interact is the immediate past, the present, and the immediate future. The bubble of time included in the immediate past, present, and future is considered "the present." The events of our lives flow past us into an ever-increasing past; the future is not normally considered. This overemphasis on the importance of the past and minimization of the importance of the future greatly complicates a basic understanding of eschatology and a hope for the world to come.

The Yoruba tribe of West Africa use a well-known curse, "Go die in the bush." This is one of the worst Yoruba curses because historically they were buried under the floor of their houses. To die away from home was the greatest shame and tragedy. According to the Yoruba worldview, people die and are buried, but they live on as living dead. Their presence and preferences are always acknowledged. Although this is certainly not taught in Bible classes, this cultural influence over the people has colored their worldview. One pastor said that the people are nominal Christians; they may be in church on Sunday but just as easily in the witch doctor's hut on Tuesday. These people live in a land that has historically embraced 401 Yoruba gods and goddesses. This worldview does not evaporate upon praying a prayer; deep discipleship and biblical teaching are needed to develop a Christian worldview and godly living.

In *Listen to the Drums*, C. F. Eaglesfield said, "The greatest need is that of providing leadership for the churches. . . . The leader in many churches is often the one who can read. His instruction is often questionable."[3] It is indeed questionable . . . to say the least! Imagine if the leaders in our churches were simply the ones who could read. Would that guarantee sound biblical instruction? Nigeria has lost funding and missionary personnel for theological education that the sending churches supplied for years. After all, Nigeria is considered reached. Some mission agencies defend this position, saying that the Nigerians already have many pastors who were trained in Nigeria as well as some who were sent to the USA and the UK to earn advanced degrees. However, these men are full-time or bi-vocational pastors and cannot serve as professors. They live all around the country (with a population of 140 million) and are nowhere near the seminary. Most of these pastors do not feel called to teach in seminary. Of course, this challenge is not found in Nigeria alone.

Missionaries in Ecuador know that the church there shares many ecclesiastical challenges with Nigeria. Many of the Ecuadorian challenges also arise from syncretism and worldview issues. Baptists have been in Ecuador since 1951. There was once a thriving Ecuadorian Baptist Theological Seminary that was training many men and women to serve the church. It was blessed with personnel, funds, material resources, and a well-appointed facility. However, the need for speed to reach the unreached people groups caused some to prefer abandoning theological education there, noting that Ecuadorian churches had received training for twenty years. They argued that twenty years should be sufficient, and the nationals should be able to train the new generations of pastors, professors, and practitioners. However, this is simply not a fair assessment. As in Nigeria, the nationals who were trained are full-time pastors, are bi-vocational, or live too far away to work at the seminary. Tragically, today over half of the Baptist churches in Ecuador have no trained pastor, and only 17 percent of the pastors in the country have received theological education and pastoral training.

I noticed the great need for such training when my family and I served as missionaries among the Highland Quichuas of the Ecuadorian Andes. The few indigenous pastors implored us to not start more churches. I wondered why, since there was an obvious need for more to be planted. They reported that there were pastors in some areas of the country who served eight, ten, or more churches, and what they really needed was more trained leaders. While conducting field research interviews among these poorest of the poor, my last question was always, "What is the greatest need among your people?" Of all the many possible answers that could have surfaced—church buildings, money, medicine, government representation, literacy, etc. —in every case the answer was pastoral and leadership training.

Peru, Ecuador's southern neighbor, also shares the need for trained pastors and leaders. I often travel to Peru to help train national pastors and church planters. On my first such trip, as I taught on basic doctrines, I reminded them of the need to share this information with others. A younger class member asked how to share these truths with preliterate people who lack the ability to read or write. As I explained basic ideas of teaching primary oral learners, an older lady in the class seemed very concerned. She asked, "What about me? Can I go to heaven when I die, too?" When she realized I was taken back by her question, she explained. "We have always been told that we could not enter into the kingdom of heaven if we could not read." Although it broke my heart to hear this, in great detail I joyfully explained that the gospel has nothing to do with one's literacy level. However, another sad reality in this encounter was when I noticed that the pastors in the room were straining to hear the "correct" answer to that question.

The lady mentioned above is a sincere believer who opened her humble home for a new house church in her community. She serves and worships the Lord Jesus but lacks anyone to teach her His Word. A pastor from one of the most prolific denominations in Peru told me that his denomination lacks trained pastors for 90 percent of their churches. The other brothers told me that over half of the evangelical churches in the country lack trained pastors. These are dear brothers and sisters who love the Lord and each other, but they need trained leadership among them.

Meanwhile, some mission agencies are promoting the idea that pastors do not need theological education. It slows down the work of church planting if you must provide a trained pastor for each church. At first, this sounds logical and seems to make perfect sense. However, many missionaries today are relearning a hard lesson from missions history: When your church growth outstrips your trained leadership, you are in trouble; weak and dysfunctional churches abound.

Those who serve in theological education, as well as those who aspire to do so, have heard many reasons why we should reduce training to the nationals. Some have said, "Places like Nigeria, Ecuador, and Peru do not need any help; they have the Bible and the Holy Spirit to guide them into all truth. They already have the people that we have trained who ought to do the training for the others in their countries, and besides, they might become dependent upon us if we continue to provide their training. They must learn to do this for themselves." Consider some responses to this argument, offered by missionaries who have seen the problems that result from neglecting Paul's instruction in 2 Timothy 2:2, "And what you have heard from me in the presence of many witnesses entrust to faithful men who will be able to teach others also."

"Places like Nigeria, Ecuador, and Peru do not need any help; they have the Bible and the Holy Spirit to guide them into all truth."

It is neither responsible nor accurate to say that a Bible and the Holy Spirit is all someone needs. Many dogmatic preachers are genuinely saved and have a Bible, but they see in the Bible only what they want to see. Many well-meaning but untaught brothers are wrongly interpreting the Bible and leading people astray. All of us appreciate the training that we have received and realize that we have been taught truths that we may never have seen for ourselves—or at least not for many years.

"Places like Nigeria, Ecuador, and Peru already have the pastors whom we have trained, and they ought to do the training now for the others in their countries."

The ones who have been trained through the years are those who were called into the ministry. Seminaries did not consciously, intentionally, or proactively train professors; they trained pastors. No one should fault these pastors for remaining true to their calling. It is true that some of them would be glad to help if they could, but they are overwhelmed with their pastorates and family responsibilities—especially those who are serving as bi-vocational pastors, as denominational workers, or in other ministries. Many do not live near their country's seminary locations and could not logistically manage such a responsibility.

"Places like Nigeria, Ecuador, and Peru might become dependent upon us if we continue to provide their training. They must learn to do this for themselves."

Dependency is a complicated problem that should be avoided with all due diligence. Yet, generally, dependency refers to financial matters. Some have extrapolated this concept to apply to training as well. While we do not want the national church to depend on our training forever, it is never right to stop training without first training the trainers who will replace us.

For instance, when an agency decides to no longer direct a bookstore ministry and hands the keys to the nationals with no training to prepare them, missionaries should not be surprised when the bookstore suffers. I have had the uncomfortable experience of translating a collection agency letter from a United States–based Christian publisher to a Christian bookstore in Latin America. The nationals did not know how to manage the store, buy books, pay bills, or read collection agency letters. They had simply received the keys from well-meaning missionaries who never trained them to do the work. This same approach has been applied to handing off seminaries and Bible colleges. Of course, nationals will be dependent on those already instructed and trained for their instruction and training. Discipleship and mentoring by very definition depend on knowledgeable guides who have more wisdom, life experience, and training than those whom they are guiding.

The only way to ensure that the national churches are not dependent on outside missionaries forever is not for them to step out of the picture, but rather to be obedient to 2 Timothy 2:2. We must train trainers, teach teachers, and disciple disciplers. It is clear that national churches should not become dependent on our money, but Jesus commands us to teach. Yes, we have taught them for years, but before we leave, we must teach others to teach so that they can continue the task.

The national church must have a seat at the table in the hermeneutical community. They alone have the emic perspective that is essential for a proper contextualization of the gospel. However, until nationals are biblically and theologically trained, missionaries must provide the proper parameters in the grammatico-historical interpretation process as well as critical contextualization. The reality is that many mission agencies have left the table.

GLOBAL NEEDS

An alarming reality in global Christianity today coincides with the abandonment of thorough theological preparation of the churches we have reached. Without understanding this sobering new reality, some may be tempted to simply shake their heads and feel pity for these benighted brothers teaching heresy in other lands. The reality is that there are now many more Christians in what is called the Southern Church than in the traditional sending countries.

The Southern Church refers to Africa, Asia, and the nations south of the Rio Grande in the Americas. The church is growing exponentially in these countries. They not only outnumber those from the United States of America in numbers of Christians and churches, they send more missionaries than the United States and Western Europe combined. Sadly, their lack of theological education, pastoral preparation, and leadership training is reflected in the aberrant forms of Christianity found in their lands.

Philip Jenkins has noted this phenomenon of growth in the Southern Church in his book *The Next Christendom: The Coming of Global Christianity.* He writes, "Over the past century . . . the center of gravity has shifted inexorably southward, to Africa, Asia, and Latin

America. Already today, the largest Christian communities on the planet are to be found in Africa and Latin America. If we want to visualize a 'typical' contemporary Christian, we should think of a woman living in a village in Nigeria or in a Brazilian favela."[4] Christopher Wright also writes about this reality in his book *The Mission of God*, "From a situation at the beginning of the twentieth century when approximately 90 percent of all the world's Christians lived in the West or North (i.e., predominantly Europe and North America), the beginning of the twenty-first century finds at least 75 percent of the world's Christians in the continents of the South and East—Latin America, Africa and parts of Asia and the Pacific."[5]

This trend is a new phenomenon because for the first time in centuries there are more Christians in other parts of the world than there are in Europe and North America. The Western church now sits in the shadow of the Southern Church, the massive younger big brother in global Christianity. Of course, this fantastic growth rate is not the alarming reality. We give praise for this answer to our prayers and missionary efforts. The alarming aspect is that there has been a concomitant growth of aberrant doctrine and bizarre practice in the Southern Church.

In an article in *The Economist* magazine, Harvard professor Harvey Cox points out the reasons why syncretistic Pentecostalism has grown so quickly around the world. He says, "One is the fact that it reconnects people with primitive religion: it taps into a deep substratum of primal spirituality, filling the 'ecstasy deficit' left by cooler religions. The movement's emphasis on experience rather than doctrine gives it a remarkable ability to absorb other faiths, from spirit possession in the Caribbean to ancestor worship in Africa, from folk healing in Brazil to shamanism in Korea. As the Pentecostals say, 'the man with an experience is never at the mercy of the man with a doctrine.' The other is that Pentecostalism offers a 'third way' between scientific rationalism and traditional religion."[6] Failure to understand existing folk religions and the cultural nuances of world religions in their various contexts has resulted in startling degrees of syncretism in many places.[7]

Nature abhors a vacuum, and human beings do not like the tension of questions with no answers. When a people embrace Christianity and begin to explore its implications, they must have biblical answers. In the absence of biblical answers, the answers to questions such as, "Why did my daughter die?" or, "How can I ensure crop success?" will be answered with the former traditional religions.

If we are not training national believers to believe biblically sound Christian doctrine and to interpret the Word of God correctly, the day will soon come when those who represent Christ in this world will be preaching a gospel that Jesus never gave. When people wonder what Christianity is about, they will look to a "typical" Christian. The person they look to will not be a Christian in a Western evangelical church preaching a gospel that orthodox, biblical Christianity will recognize. Doctrinally sound New Testament Christianity is shrinking in size and influence.

Mission agencies have withheld human and financial resources for theological education in order to speed the work of exponential church growth among the nationals and to avoid all forms of dependency. Those who sense the fallacy in such a methodology sometimes shrug and turn back to their books while confidently reminding themselves that at least Western Christians have the truth. The day is rapidly approaching when few beyond our theologically sound Western seminaries and churches will care. Global Christianity is growing in such a way that truth is considered to be that which works; pragmatism rules in the absence of propositional truth. We will have to say in that day that we did not lose our voice; we willingly yielded it. If trends continue, we will one day shout truth in order to rebuke, reprove, exhort, instruct, and correct, only to be considered irrelevant and not be heard.

CONCLUSION

The Great Commission is not just about witnessing or church planting. Jesus said to make disciples of the ethnic groups of the world, and to do so by teaching them to observe all that He commanded us.

We must not relegate pastoral training, theological education, and biblical teaching to a level of less important missions activity when they are a primary and necessary means for the fulfilling of the Great Commission. Right now, people all over the world are begging for help. They want teaching, Bible training, theological education, and pastoral preparation in Nigeria, Ecuador, Peru, and, of course, in many other countries. Right now, we still have a voice. May it ring out for the glory of God and the advance of the gospel.

SUGGESTED READING

Cox, Harvey. "Christianity Reborn," *The Economist*. December 23, 2006, 48–50.

Eaglesfield, C. F. *Listen to the Drums*. Nashville: Broadman and Holman Publishers, 1950.

Hiebert, Paul G., R. Daniel Shaw, and Tite Tiénou. *Understanding Folk Religion: A Christian Response to Popular Beliefs and Practices*. Grand Rapids: Baker Books, 1999.

Jenkins, Philip. *The New Faces of Christianity: Believing the Bible in the Global South*. Oxford: Oxford University Press, 2006.

_____. *The Next Christendom: The Coming of Global Christianity*. Oxford: Oxford University Press, 2002.

Wright, Christopher J. H. *The Mission of God: Unlocking the Bible's Grand Narrative*. Downers Grove, IL: InterVarsity Press, 2006.

2

MISSIONARIES TRAINING NATIONALS: HOW MUCH IS ENOUGH?

It is undeniable that mission agencies and the missionaries they send often emphasize strategies that call for unbelievable speed. Theological education, pastoral preparation, and leadership training—once seen to be essential for establishing a mature indigenous church—are increasingly regarded as no longer relevant. In fact, when speaking of the time necessary to train local leadership in biblical and theological studies as a hindrance to speed, the architect of a modern strategy for church planting movements said, "Higher education may benefit church leaders at some point, but it can hinder a Church Planting Movement in its early stages."[1] Furthermore, he has responded to the suggestion that such church planting movements are seen by many as "fertile ground for heresy," saying, "This may be true, but it is not necessarily so. The often-proposed solution is more theological training. However, church history has shown that the cure can be worse than the disease. Since the first theological school at Alexandria, Egypt, seminaries have proven themselves capable of transmitting heresy as well as sound doctrine. The same is true today."[2] Apparently this is sufficient reason to abandon formal, systematic, and thorough training of nationals. Instead, the method utilized in place of traditional training models focuses on training nationals only in Church Planting Movement methodology.

When speed becomes the driving force and heartbeat of a strategy, and expediency rules decision making, nonessentials are jettisoned as impediments to progress. Imagine two boats to illustrate this idea. One is a loaded freighter that sits low in the water and travels slowly as it plows the ocean carrying heavy cargo to waiting ports. By stark contrast, the other is a modern jet boat that virtually flies across the surface of the water, barely touching it, but covering long distances in the twinkle of an eye. The freighter represents the way that many view "old school" missions. It sits low in the water and moves slowly because of all it carries. Those who embrace this perspective see this missionary model as irresponsible, rather than just too slow. Many believe that the jet boat represents a better missionary model, as it allows covering more ground more quickly— and that should be the primary goal. Any model that impedes rapid advance is viewed negatively. However, the jet boat does little more than cover territory; the freighter delivers the needed supplies.

Contemporary mission strategies emphasize reaching, preaching to, and leaving as many people groups as possible as fast as possible. In fact, the contemporary focus on speed influences all areas of missionary life and work. The qualifications and requirements for those who are to be sent as missionaries are also relaxed when speed is the highest value. Requiring missionary candidates to have college or seminary degrees slows down the agencies' efforts to get missionaries to all the UPGs. Streamlining the missionary force results in a streamlining of the missionary task in many mission agencies. Some agencies have charged missionaries to target a UPG, get them "reached," and leave within three, five, or seven years. Since this leaves insufficient time to learn the language, culture, and worldview, the task of missions is necessarily redefined. When missionaries or agency heads are reminded of the Great Commission duty to remain long enough to make disciples and teach them, they will often respond in frustration that they *have* taught them and ask, "How much is enough?"

CONSIDERING THE TASK

The missionary task is not easy or neat and refuses to fit on a prescribed timeline. How long missionaries should continue training the target fields is not really the best way to define the task. Thus, asking when missionaries may consider their efforts to be enough so they may move on is the wrong question. Better questions are, "What is it that missionaries are to do?" and, "What is the task of international missions?" How the missionary task is defined and understood will drive the strategies and methodologies of mission agencies and their missionaries.

THE AMOUNT OF TIME that a missionary remains in a people group training nationals can vary depending on his or her adaptation to the culture, grasp of the language, love for the people, gifting for training, style of teaching, degree of welcome in the host culture, and sense of God's leading. A person could come for a few classes, a few years, or a lifetime. The longer a person stays, the more capable he or she becomes of really communicating deeply, and if the person who has come is a godly and loving person, he or she can teach, encourage, and stand behind local peers for a lifetime, resulting in a tremendous harvest.

—WORKER IN CHINA

In all fairness, some mission agencies remind us that they have been faithfully training nationals for many decades as one of their primary methodologies. However, these agencies have found that as the missions world turned its attention to reaching unreached people groups, missionary candidates and financial donors followed. Reaching the unreached is what seems to be exciting and the cutting edge of missions for many churches, missionary candidates, and financial donors. Consequently, many agencies have shifted from their traditional fields of service and methodologies in order to be seen as relevant and viable.

Reducing the task of international missions to reaching, preaching, and leaving as many as possible is irresponsible. Such an understanding of the missionary task spawns new definitions. A "reached people group" becomes any group that has at least 2 percent of its population self-identifying as evangelical Christians. If we reduce the goal of missions to simply "reaching the unreached," then anyone who lives and works among a group that is two-percent-plus-one-evangelical cannot be considered a missionary who cares about advancing the kingdom of God. New definitions hold that an entire people group of millions of souls may be considered "engaged" if someone somewhere claims to be trying to start a church among them. "Preaching the gospel" can mean relating the message in culturally inappropriate ways through an interpreter—regardless of whether it is truly understood by the hearer or not. A "church" can mean nothing more than a group of people who have gathered together at the invitation of the missionary. A wise maxim in missions is "Your ecclesiology will drive your missiology." That is, what you believe a church to be will drive everything you do in missions.

TEACHING THEM

As we continue to ask what tasks and duties biblical missions includes, we cannot avoid the teaching component. Many feel that since they have already taught the nationals for years, they should not have to continue teaching them. There are really two main ideas to consider. First, how long must we continue to teach them before moving elsewhere? Second, how much training is enough? For now, let us consider the question of how long missionaries should continue to dedicate themselves to the task of training the nationals. We will address the second question in chapter 3.

LOGICAL PERSPECTIVE

The argument in favor of streamlining the task and adopting a jet boat approach to international missions seems a logical solution to the challenge of reaching all the UPGs in the world as quickly as possible. We live in a world of entrepreneurs who solve business challenges with a "can do" attitude. International diplomats negotiate peace treaties and resolve differences between nations. The World Health Organization can predict the time until diseases will be eradicated with calculated precision. Weekly sitcoms present crises that are easily handled in the space of a thirty-minute time slot—even allowing time for commercials. What is the crisis that evangelicals face? It is that there is a world filled with people who will die and go to hell unless they hear the gospel and are born again. That is a huge problem, and we are trying to solve it as fast as possible.

As modernists who seek practical answers to real problems, we sit down with maps, demographic tables, and lists of agencies to plot our strengths, weaknesses, risks, and opportunities. Considering the challenge, we put the best minds to work to meet it. It seems obvious that the best way to meet the challenge is to preach the gospel everywhere as fast as we can. Once a group has been reached, why would we leave someone behind to teach the next generation when we still have not reached the rest of the world? A part of the answer to this question lies in another question that should precede it—why do we go to the nations at all?

DEFINING OBEDIENCE

Some would maintain that we go to the nations to preach the gospel out of obedience to the Great Commission. Their cry is that we should make Christ's last command our first priority. Others maintain that we are to go in order to rescue the perishing. After all, if we do not go, they will not hear the gospel; and if they do not even hear, they will most certainly enter into a Christless eternity when they die. I believe that overarching both of these reasons is the desire to glorify God. The Westminster Catechism teaches us that the chief end of man is to glorify God and to enjoy Him forever. Yet, if this is our goal, then we should do the work He has given us to do in the way that He has told us to do it. The commands to disciple, teach, mentor, and guide those who come behind us are found throughout the Old and New Testaments. However, as we have seen, many are often frustrated, sincerely believing that "teaching them" slows down the work of missions rather than enables it. I suggest that this is only because they have narrowly defined the task of missions as reaching and preaching to every people group. There is no need to dichotomize reaching and teaching as if they were mutually exclusive efforts. The Lord has clearly included both in His instructions to His church.

When missionaries dichotomize reaching and teaching, the result is that one is always prioritized over the other. Eventually, the lesser is considered to be so secondary that, when the streamlining begins, it is relegated to a category that is not real missionary work. Indeed, it is often then seen to impede the real work of missions. Such thinking has resulted in a missions force that consists of any willing person who can go and share a gospel tract. The 1 Timothy 3:1–7 qualifications for Christian ministers are the first to be set aside in the streamlining as too demanding and limiting. Then, ministry experience—once thought to be essential for both missionary preparation and the demonstration of ministry skills—is seen as unnecessary. After all, missionaries will receive all the experience they need when they are missionaries on the field. Soon afterward, the requirement that candidates have Bible or theological training is set aside for pragmatic reasons; when agencies demand that candidates spend time obtaining this training it delays their deployment to the field. Educational preparation could also result in their becoming encumbered with unsecured debt, student loans, or other life entanglements that would preclude missionary service. Certainly, requiring ministry experience increases the risk that students serving as pastors would sense a burden for their flocks and stay stateside; many others fall in love with the American dream and never leave.

Other agencies have lowered the qualifications for missionary candidates based upon ministry reasons rather than pragmatic reasons. Some have argued that a missionary does not need a theological education to share an evangelistic tract or present the gospel. Yet, sharing a tract is not all that missionaries do. The only things new believers know about the gospel, theology, and sound doctrine are what come out of the missionary's mouth. Missionaries form the theology of the new believers. When missionaries can do little more than share a tract, the new believers often blend the few things they learn about Christ into their traditional religions and worldview.

Many agencies have reduced their strategies and methodologies to include little more than initial gospel presentations, and training beyond that level is seen as superfluous. However, since missionaries are the new believers' only source of knowledge about Christ and Christian theology, what will the missionaries teach if they are not prepared? James P. Boyce, founding president of The Southern Baptist Theological Seminary, said in a speech at Furman University in 1856, "The results of past missionary efforts appear to indicate that we, like the apostles, must adopt the system of home laborers, if we would evangelize the world. We must get natives to proclaim the glad tidings of salvation. The men whom we send forth to missionary stations must then be qualified to instruct the native preachers in all the elements of theological education. They will not only have to put the Bible into their hands as a textbook, but they will have to prepare, in the native language, or translate into it such books of theology, as shall give them adequate instruction."[3]

Sending missionaries who have the lowest common denominators of ministry skills and preparation may boost the number of missionaries, but it will also decimate the percentage of missionaries who are qualified to pastor, teach, or preach. David Allen Bledsoe has rightly emphasized that as necessary as theological preparation of missionaries may be, it is not enough; missionaries also need to know the cultures where they will serve. He writes, "No doubt, the historic mission fields are not identical copies of the West. The target people of these countries have their own language, history, and world view. Partnering will necessitate research and time for the professor-missionary to understand and help present biblical solutions that are culturally meaningful."[4]

MISSIONS STRATEGY

A phenomenon of modern missions that influences every denomination and mission agency is what Ralph Winter calls the amateurization of missions.[5] Missionaries on the field are receiving increasing numbers of short-term missionaries and mission teams and must constantly find new ways to use them. The hundreds of thousands of church members who go out as short-term missionaries are changing the way many view missions. One relatively new approach that is growing in popularity utilizes the USA-based church as the sole missionary to a region or people in other countries. The church adopts an area where there is little or no evangelical witness and agrees to take several short-term mission trips there per year. Increasingly, these stateside churches are working in areas where there is no missionary. The church actually becomes the only missionary reaching out to an unchurched area. This is at once laudable and insufficient.

On one hand, the churches will be able to evangelize areas that have not had anyone to do so. However, there is no missionary on the field to follow up with these "converts." The churches who come lack not only cultural awareness but also language skills, and they are forced to work through interpreters who may not share evangelical beliefs with the mission team. On subsequent trips, there is usually no way to locate and disciple those who were converted on previous trips. This strategy is tantamount to starting a business in a country where you do not live and only visit a few times per year, one week at a time. These efforts are an excellent way to include churches in the USA in kingdom advance, but they must find ways to fulfill the Great Commission—they must work to make disciples and teach them to observe all that He has commanded.

A similar emphasis is the role of church-based teams assisting missionaries in their ministries through the use of short-term mission trips. Many churches include short-term mission projects as a major component of their missions ministry. Some of their trips are very helpful to the missionaries on the field. They may conduct survey work, distribute literature, or open doors into new communities with medical and dental clinics. Other teams build church buildings, homes for pastors, or school buildings. They dig wells or help with relief work after natural disasters. No one should deny the kingdom value of these trips, especially when they are in conjunction with career missionaries who receive the teams, orient them for culturally appropriate interaction, and follow up on their efforts. However, the crucial element that is almost always lacking is continued discipleship and training for the new believers. When preparing annual budgets, many churches are hesitant to designate missions funds for theological education on the field when doing so would reduce available funds for sending their own members on future mission trips.

Some short-term mission team members and long-term missionaries see the winning of souls as the primary goal of missions. When isolated from the broader biblical task that Jesus gave and Paul modeled, this one-dimensional strategy of winning souls is too simplistic. Additionally, it sometimes results in an "end justifies the means" mentality. Some present the gospel with heavy-handed, manipulative persuasion techniques that seek to trick people into praying a prayer. Others unintentionally cause confusion when they do not understand that some cultures would never tell a guest something that offends or contradicts the guest's beliefs. Many in these cultures will pray a prayer as the presenter obviously desires, simply to please and avoid offending the presenter. This is why returning mission teams may report hundreds of decisions for Christ in a one-week trip when faithful missionaries serving there have not seen twenty conversions in their entire ministry. Still, whatever it takes to get the decision—and as many decisions as possible—is what drives some missionaries and their strategies.

How do these same missionaries interpret the Great Commission's admonishment to make disciples and, more pointedly, to teach them to observe all that Christ commanded us? A leader in one agency was asked how he interpreted those components of Christ's commands when newly adopted strategies and methodologies reflected a decision to abandon efforts in theological education and training. He responded that they had determined to interpret those commands affectively. He meant that they would win people to the Lord, and as they were leaving encourage them to observe all that Christ has commanded; they would just not be staying around to teach them what that means or how to do it. That would certainly allow the missionaries to move on shortly after some nationals pray to receive Christ.

How Long Is Long Enough?

In many countries of the world, such as Nigeria (as discussed in the first chapter), theological education has been a primary ministry of mission agencies for decades. Countless dollars and man-hours have been invested in buildings, books, pianos, and patient instruction in virtually every discipline of the theological encyclopedia. It seems to be a never-ending process. A weary missionary in these countries might add the theological training of nationals to the list of things in Proverbs 30:15b–16 that are always lacking.[6] However, most would agree that simply because the task seems never-ending, that is not a sound, logical argument to stop doing it. Countless believers have heard the gospel, raised their hand, and joined a church, but lack trained pastors to train them in the Word. Missionaries feeling the pressure or burden to move on to the next group are concerned with the plight of these new believers, but the question still hangs in the air, "How long is long enough?"

Shift the question to another context. When should a pastor consider his work of preaching, discipling, and counseling church members to be over? Those who were members when he began his ministry will seek his wisdom and counsel for the rest of their lives. They will have crises of health, child rearing, finances, and faith. Can he ever say that he has finished the task? No, there will always be the perennial issues with existing members as well as the new believers who come to the Lord through his ministry. In the life of every one of them, the process of teaching, discipling, mentoring, and counseling begins afresh.

Think of it this way. How long should a medical training school continue its task? Will there ever be a time that a hospital board of directors will issue a press release declaring that all the physicians who should be trained are now graduated and in practice? What about all these graduated physicians; will they reach the point of finishing their work? Will the day ever come that one can say that the residents of his city are in perfect health and that his work is done?

AUTHORITY AND INFLUENCE

Will there ever be a day when a parent is finished parenting and advising? Sadly for some, but gladly for most, that day never comes. The parents' role will change throughout the lives of their children, but their responsibility, input, and influence should never come to an end. The following diagram is a good way to think about the ever-changing role of a parent.

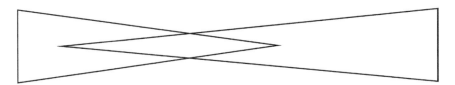

The triangle on the left represents the parent's control over the child's life. The triangle on the right represents the child's control over his or her own life. And the entire illustration—from left to right —illustrates the timeline of the child's life. In the beginning, virtually every decision that is made is the prerogative of the parent: when to eat, what to eat, what to wear, etc. Yet the day comes in the life of the child when the parent allows the child to decide whether to wear the red shirt or the blue one, whether to wear a dress or blue jeans, or whether to have toast or cereal. As the child's responsibility in daily decisions grows, the parent's control diminishes. Eventually, the parent has taught and guided the child so well that the child can responsibly make the decisions of life with little direct guidance from the parent. However, the parent should always be interested and involved in the life of the child. Additionally, there will be other children, grandchildren, nieces, and nephews who will seek counsel and guidance throughout the wise parent's life. Responsible parents would never abandon their children at the hospital when they are born, nor at any time as long as they live. Parental guidance will continue for many years, and the children will grow and mature little by little along the way. In the same way, missionaries should seek to provide oversight, insight, wisdom, counsel, teaching, and mentoring in the lives of new converts in their ministries.

Missionaries have always said that they wanted to work themselves out of a job. However, many missionaries have stayed on for entire careers in places where the church has been established. They are sometimes accused of forgetting that their task was to work themselves out of a job. It only seems that way at first glance. Others have left shortly after the first few raised their hands indicating that they wanted to accept Christ as Savior. They do not feel called to stay and disciple, so they leave to get more folks to raise their hands. Still others worked themselves out of the job of being the initial pioneer evangelist and then entered into the role of discipler. Later, they became co-laborers with national brothers and sisters. Further on, they became participants in the ministries of their former students as they started over as pioneers in a new area. Even though they have remained in the country, they are not sitting still and basking in the glow of yesterday, as it might appear.

MISSIONARY ROLES

Harold Fuller of Serving In Mission has provided this insight into the various roles of missionaries.[7] When a missionary first arrives in an unreached, unevangelized area, his role is that of pioneer. Many think of the pioneer missionary wearing a pith helmet and swinging a machete, although that is rarely the case anymore. Many new missions areas are in the heart of a modern downtown that is densely populated with high-rise apartment buildings. The pioneer missionary evangelizes and plants churches in the new area. As a core of believers comes together and forms into a local church, the pioneer missionary may find that he is more tied to the work than he may prefer. If he has a true pioneering spirit, he will feel frustration that he cannot leave these believers to grow on their own while he moves on into virgin territory to again preach Christ where He has not been named.

Sometimes the missionary witnesses individuals embracing Christianity, calls the new believers a church, leaves them to fend for themselves, and heads out to find other groups to evangelize. The resulting church is anemic at best, heretical at worst, and normally does not survive very long except when thoroughly syncretized with traditional religions. A healthier outcome results when the missionary sees his role changing into that of a parent who must nurture and mentor the young churches and disciples. In the absence of this role evolution in the life of the pioneer, he should at least endeavor to bring in a second wave of missionaries. The second role of missionary engagement is that of a parent or nurturer. Indeed, this is what many missionaries feel their call to be: discipling, training pastors, teaching theology, forming training schools, and helping indigenous believers establish culturally appropriate forms of Christianity. As these believers and churches mature and reproduce, the missionary will see a shift in role once again.

The third missionary role is the partner missionary. This missionary works shoulder to shoulder with trained national evangelists, pastors, and professors. They share the work and the decisions, and they expand and develop the ministry in that context. Again, the missionary who came in as pioneer but has since shifted to being a parent may feel the discomfort of growing pains throughout the process. Alternately, if he believes that moving on is the best way to be faithful to God's call on his life, he should leave only after he facilitates the arrival of new missionaries to assume this role.

The fourth role is participant; this adjustment is called for when the work continues to progress in an area. Eventually, the missionary should be only a participant in the nationals' ministry. Normally, this development in the relationship is realized when the missionary begins to work in new areas. He will visit the old work from time to time and enjoy the preaching ministry of pastors who came to faith years ago under his own ministry.

In areas where this role shifting does not occur, there is often dysfunction and tension. Missionaries who do not understand the need to hand the ministry to discipled nationals continue in their original roles. The first generation of believers may actually prefer that they do so and virtually demand that the missionaries continue in their original roles. The second and third generations of believers begin to wonder why the missionaries continue to "lord" their authority over them, especially when they reflect on the fact that their parents and grandparents are believers. They may wonder why this missionary who still does not speak their language perfectly or does not totally understand their culture is viewed as a prince among his subjects. Cries of, "Missionary, go home!" tend to bubble out of this pot. Understanding the varied roles of legitimate missions and one's personal call to missions is the key to finding peace, balance, and fruitful ministry in the midst of shifting needs and demands on the mission field.

China has been a focal point of missions success in recent decades and is sometimes heralded as an example of what can be done when Westerners get out of the way. The house church growth in the country has been both explosive and encouraging. Yet, all is not as well as we might hope; China's church is hurting in many ways because of the dearth of theologically trained leaders. Missionaries report that evangelicals in China are losing ten thousand house churches every year to cults because their church leaders have no theological training. They cannot teach or defend what orthodox Christianity holds to be true. Prior to the expulsion of Western missionaries, Chinese churches had learned how to evangelize, but not trained trainers or prepared professors since few had expected to be forced out. After the revolution, many of the Chinese pastors who had been biblically qualified and trained among them were imprisoned or killed. The churches continued to evangelize, which along with the persecution brought rapid growth, but not many knew sound theology and there was nowhere to learn it. One missionary reports that Chinese churches know how to do evangelism, but they do not know much more than that.

CONCLUSION

When one asks the question, "How long should missionaries continue teaching?" the answer should be, "Which missionary?" Those who have been called to disciple, teach, train, equip, and mentor should do so until the Lord changes their gifting and calling. Those called to pioneer ministries will always feel understandably frustrated if they are tied down in a ministry that they are not gifted, called, or desiring to do. There are various stages of missions work and there are diverse gifts and callings. The biblical commands to both evangelize and teach disciples should obliterate efforts and arguments to relegate everything after the pioneer stage to a lesser role and value in missions.

"Teaching them" is draining, time-consuming, messy, and all too often heartbreaking. Almost all missionaries have felt more than once that it would be so much easier to move on and start over in another place. They wonder, "Does the role of training, teaching, and mentoring really have to continue forever?" Perhaps a good way to answer the question with which we began the chapter is to ask ourselves what the church in the target context should look like when our work is done. That is, what is the end vision for the work? Do we long to see a healthy church that knows and rightly interprets God's Word, applying it appropriately in the culture? Do we hope to see theologically trained, biblically qualified leaders in the churches, who evangelize, disciple, and pastor others in the people group? Is the goal to see a church that can continue the work of reaching and teaching their fellow nationals and discipling the converts until Jesus returns? If so, then we cannot possibly step away from the work after the initial acceptance of Christ, telling ourselves that they have the Holy Spirit and He will lead them into all truth. There is hard work to be done, and it needs to be done for a long time before missionaries can leave new churches and believers alone.

In recent decades, as the focus has shifted from traditional fields and ministries to more exotic locations and UPGs, many missionaries finally have seen the need to hand the work to the nationals. Unfortunately, they often handed the keys to nationals who had never been trained. Although the missionary may identify young men willing to lead the churches, are these churches ready to be left in their hands? Sadly, when missionaries later learn that the church buildings are in disrepair, the Christian bookstore shelves are empty, the seminary is closed, and the feeding stations are out of food, they blame the national church. Only rarely does a missionary realize that he asked his brothers to do something he had never trained them to do. In many situations, Western missionary ministries were completely dependent upon Western missionary funds that left when the missionary did. We set the nationals up for failure and blamed them when it happened.

The solution is to continue to train leaders until you have trained people who not only understand for themselves, but they know how to train others to train others. How much is enough? How long should missionaries continue to teach? The answer is as simple as it is biblical. Don't stop teaching until you have taught teachers; don't stop training until you have trained trainers.

SUGGESTED READING

Smallman, William H. *Able to Teach Others Also: Nationalizing Global Ministry Training.* Salt Lake City: Mandate Press, 2001.

Fuller, W. Harold. *Mission-Church Dynamics.* Pasadena, CA: William Carey Library, 1980.

Winter, Ralph. "The Editorial of Ralph D. Winter." *Mission Frontiers* 18 (March/April 1996).

3
THE BARE MINIMUM: WHAT MUST WE TEACH?

Let us now turn our attention to a logical follow-up question to "How long must missionaries continue to teach?" That question is, "What do the nationals have to know before missionaries leave them?" or, "What is the lowest common denominator of Christian knowledge— the bare minimum of theological understanding—that churches in the majority world must have before missionaries should move on?"

The missionary's task is to continue the work of teaching and training until the national church is thoroughly equipped for continuing the propagation of the gospel and sound doctrine without the assistance of others. Yet, what does that look like? Paul told Timothy in 2 Timothy 2:2, "And what you have heard from me in the presence of many witnesses entrust to faithful men who will be able to teach others also." One might still wonder, "What things that we heard from you, Paul?" He also wrote to Titus about the importance of ensuring that doctrinally instructed godly leaders be in place in all the churches.

This is why I left you in Crete, so that you might put what re-
mained into order, and appoint elders in every town as I directed
you—if anyone is above reproach, the husband of one wife, and his
children are believers and not open to the charge of debauchery or
insubordination. For an overseer, as God's steward, must be above
reproach. He must not be arrogant or quick-tempered or a drunk-
ard or violent or greedy for gain, but hospitable, a lover of good,
self-controlled, upright, holy, and disciplined. He must hold firm to
the trustworthy word as taught, so that he may be able to give
instruction in sound doctrine and also to rebuke those who con-
tradict it. (Titus 1:5–9)

However, this still leaves missionaries asking the practical question
of how much education is sufficient.

Another way to approach the matter is to ask, "What will the finished product look like?" Assuming that the day comes when missionaries may wave good-bye to the pastor(s) in their ministry and
go to a new field of service, what will the church waving back at
them look like? Clearly answering that question provides the missionary an essential reference point.

Any wise and effective strategy should anticipate the end goal. As
you begin to formulate a strategy to meet the end goal of the missionary task, look at where you are standing and answer the question, "Where am I now?" Consider the current spiritual condition
and circumstances of the believers you are leading. Then lift your
eyes to the horizon and ask, "Where do I want to end up? What kind
of church do I hope to leave behind at the end of my ministry here?"
Next, plot the steps on the path from where you are to where you
want to be. You will be wise to consider potential problems, challenges, the projected timeline, resources available now, and those
resources that will be necessary in order to finish. Then, as you begin
to implement your plan, stop along the way at predetermined incre-
ments to assess your progress and adjust your plan if necessary.

For instance, if you are an evangelist and church planter, you will
first need to learn the language and nuances of the culture in order

to clearly communicate the gospel message. Once the people begin to come to Christ, you will begin the process of discipleship and establishing churches among them. Then the question arises, "When should I leave and begin again elsewhere?" A need for speed may nudge you out of the nest before your "offspring" are ready to fly on their own. Instead, you must teach them how to evangelize, disciple, and train church leadership—or see that someone has adopted this as their end goal—before you leave. God has charged the church-planting missionary to teach the people sufficiently so that "the man of God may be competent, equipped for every good work" (2 Timothy 3:17).

IDENTIFYING THE PROBLEM

What is the essential biblical and theological knowledge that God's Word requires church leaders to have? What ministry skills are nonnegotiable? What character issues should you look for and develop in the national leadership? How can national pastors learn all of this in the absence of seminaries? How can you ensure that they can replicate the process before you leave?

Many countries do not have national seminaries or pastoral training programs available for all their languages and cultures. In such situations, one tool that many missionaries are putting to good use goes by the acrostic MAWL (*model, assist, watch,* and *leave*). The MAWL training model is a method to educate disciples by following the example of medical doctors and pastors in previous centuries. It calls for the apprentice to learn from a master by watching and doing. When the apprentice is ready, he begins to do the work with the master watching and assisting him, rather than the apprentice assisting the master. The master simply watches and ensures that the apprentice is sound in knowledge and practice. When the apprentice is "soloing" without incident, the master may leave. This is an excellent model for discipleship and teaching that avoids the necessity of residential colleges and seminaries. However, this model is rarely employed to its fullest extent, and it often seeks only to train nationals to repeat the church planting experience, not giving them the thorough biblical knowledge and sound doctrinal grounding that they need.

"I WANT TO KNOW what you will be teaching us," David said to me in an extremely unfriendly tone in the midst of a group I was about to begin teaching on the mission field. He continued, "I have been a Christian for six years, and I still don't know the fundamentals." He proceeded to read to me from his French Bible, "For when for the time ye ought to be teachers, ye have need that one teach you again which [are] the first principles of the oracles of God" (Hebrews 5:12).

Then he continued, "I am supposed to have a foundation by now. I have no foundation. Do you intend to teach me the fundamentals? My church has not taught me the basics."

My wife and I had prayed for one year for twelve people into whose lives we could pour ourselves. There they sat, twelve exactly. I was dumbfounded. I asked myself once again, "What are the fundamentals?"

—DAN SHEARD

Senior Pastor, Calvary Missionary Baptist Church
Adjunct Instructor, Lincoln University

Believers and their leaders must be taught sound doctrine based on the whole counsel of the Word of God if they are to live godly lives, avoid error, and survive the onslaughts of spiritual warfare. Centuries of animism and world religions have saturated the world-views and cultures of people groups and blinded them to a biblical understanding of life. Many new believers try to understand God and what Christ has done for them against the backdrop of their former beliefs, resulting in syncretism and heresy. Their traditional understanding of reality does not evaporate upon praying a prayer. Hoyt Lovelace writes, "Immediate conversion and regeneration does happen from an initial hearing of the gospel, but in these cases, it becomes imperative that there is proper follow-up and the development of an adequately knowledgeable community of faith. Otherwise, the resultant body could be similar to a mass movement that gets together to discuss their ideas of cultural and religious change, somewhat divorced from the Truth of God."[1]

The common argument that it is sufficient for new believers to have only the Bible and the Holy Spirit, who will lead them into all truth (John 16:13), takes Jesus' words out of context. Jesus did not mean that we should not have to disciple and teach; that would be a direct contradiction to many other admonitions in the Bible that command us to do so. Jesus meant that the Holy Spirit would reveal truths in the New Testament writings yet to come. The full verse makes Jesus' meaning easier to see: "When the Spirit of truth comes, he will guide you into all the truth, for he will not speak on his own authority, but whatever he hears he will speak, and he will declare to you the things that are to come." This is clearly not permission from Jesus to abandon biblical instructions to disciple and teach.

Even in the USA, there are many believers who have the Holy Spirit and Bibles but have unfortunately imagined and embraced heresy. How much more of a danger is it to abandon those who have indicated an interest in Christ but are steeped in cultures with false religions! Missionaries who are adequately preparing national leaders should not be viewed to be slowing down the work, but rather grounding it on a solid foundation. David Bledsoe writes,

> A professor-missionary committed to church growth simultaneously strives to take his discipline, whether evangelism, theology, or biblical studies, to the thousands of people who walk by, live around, and die near his classroom. He cannot hope that his students make the application. He needs to show the connection through modeling and challenging his students to plant, assist, and pastor mission-impacting churches. Professor-missionaries

who teach their disciplines with a church growth ethos are desperately needed among established evangelical denominations in historic mission fields.[2]

A HOLISTIC APPROACH

William Carey saw the wisdom of a holistic training ministry for the nationals in his missionary strategy. His efforts to prepare pastors went beyond Bible training and theology to include many aspects that would enable leaders to help themselves and their churches. A pastor with the culturally appropriate skills for social interaction, family leadership, and wisdom for daily life is an effective leader whom the others will respect.

Quichua evangelical leaders in the Andes stated that their greatest need was leadership training. They believed that the needed training should be holistic and include more than just Bible and theology if they were to win the others in their culture. Thorough pastoral preparation ideally includes a variety of skills and knowledge for leadership. Missionaries who desire to move on to begin afresh in a new ministry location need to ensure that there is trained, biblically qualified leadership among the national churches before they leave. The bare minimum necessary for national pastors requires holistic preparation of their heads, hands, and hearts.

The Head

The task of international missions incorporates the missionary message—the gospel—at every level. The gospel is a message that teaches that God is holy, man is sinful, Jesus is the answer, and you must repent and be born again. Failure to understand the basic gospel message has often resulted in syncretism, extrabiblical requirements, or misunderstanding biblical teachings about salvation and other elements of the Christian faith. For instance, those who do not understand the gospel may believe that church membership equals salvation. When churches require a new members class, people often misunderstand the point and come to believe that since passing this course allows church membership, it also provides salvation. Another example is found where literacy has been required for communicant church members, and the ability to read and write has become requisite for salvation in the minds of people.

In order to avoid the errors of imaginative minds, believers with the Bible in their language must be taught how to interpret God's Word. The historical-grammatical method for understanding the original intent of the author is the most faithful method of interpretation, even when there is no knowledge of biblical languages. Without instruction in responsible methods of interpretation, the national pastors will lean on feelings and easily arrive at incorrect conclusions based on personal opinions. They will try to understand God's Word by viewing it through the lens of a worldview that is foreign to the Scriptures. For instance, how would a Hindu worldview understand a missionary's message containing concepts such as "eternal life" or "being born again"? What stumbling blocks would the animist experience when hearing Bible stories referring to spirits in the Bible? How would those steeped in sorcery and witchcraft view passages such as the story of Saul and the witch at Endor? Would they interpret them as affirmations of their own practice? How would ancestor worshipers view the exhortation to honor one's parents? The natural tendency is to interpret them the only way the worldview can make sense of them. A biblically responsible hermeneutical process must be in place among the leaders if the missionaries expect churches to continue in the truth.

Pastoral preparation must also include basic understanding of the message of the Bible. This does not require literacy, as even oral cultures can hear and understand the panorama of the Bible through the use of stories. Regardless of literacy level or previous education, the national pastors will greatly benefit from teaching that explains the structure of the Bible, how it was written, who the human authors were, the background of the books, themes that run throughout it, and the biblical theology that can be clearly learned from God's revelation. Imagine the people group that raised hands to accept Christ and became a church, but has learned none of these things. How long will truth continue unmixed among them?

In the absence of vast libraries filled with resources for training, some missionaries have found great value in teaching pastors how to use a doctrinally sound study Bible among those language groups where such a resource is available. One missionary provided study Bibles and taught a group of pastors how to use them to research doctrinal issues, study God's Word, prepare Bible studies and sermons, and minister to people in times of need. He left them with these study Bibles that essentially served as their pastoral libraries. More than this, he left them with confidence to study and teach the Word of God more responsibly in their ministries—something that they previously never had.

God has revealed Himself in His Word, and as such, the Bible is the only concrete absolute in the universe. Its teachings will never fail, and they are sufficient for faith and practice. Since expressions of Christianity found in many parts of the world bear little resemblance to what the Bible teaches, missionaries must bring people to the teachings of God's Word if they are to know Him rightly. God's revelation matters; the true knowledge of Him that comes through His Word is not some superfluous extra. Peter Adam has written, "We can summarize a biblical theology of preaching in these words: God has spoken, It is written, and Preach the word."[3]

Some missionaries graduate from rigorous seminary training and then go to work among cultures with low literacy levels. The process of rethinking three years of theological training that came to them in abstract conceptual forms only to present it to others in concrete narrative forms is arduous and draining. In the frustration to train leaders in such cultures, missionaries sometimes come to believe that Hebrew and Greek are not necessary skills for the national pastors. They then begin to identify other courses in the theological encyclopedia that also seem extraneous. Eventually, some missionaries believe that virtually all training is either beyond the nationals' abilities or is an unnecessary requirement for ministry.

James Engel illustrates the danger of this thinking in a fictional story based on reality. In this story, mission agency executives are celebrating the fact that the end of the Great Commission is in sight and likely to be accomplished in their lifetime. As they pore over the facts, figures, and demographics, an African woman approaches the microphone to address them:

> "I am from the country that has been considered by many of you to be the greatest example of success in world missions," she began. She told how the church was planted over a century ago, and how today 85 percent of the people call themselves Christians. Much of the growth came from evangelical and Pentecostal churches, which exceed 25 percent of the total. Excitement grew in the hall as she described high interest in Bible study and prayer. But then she asked, "Do any of you know where I am from?" Many guesses were called out, all of which were wrong. She finally said: "I am from Rwanda"—the same country in which, in 1994, 600,000 Tutsis and 400,000 Hutus died, many of them slaughtered with machetes as they huddled in churches. "In all of your zeal for evangelism, you brought us Christ but never taught us how to live." If the end is in sight, how do we explain Rwanda, as well as other so-called Christian countries where unrestrained materialism, oppression of the underprivileged, and deterioration of moral values increase annually? Surely these are not the consequences envisioned by our Lord when he said, "Go and make disciples . . . teaching them to obey everything I have commanded you" (Matthew 28:18–20).[4]

Statistics from the same period as the genocide indicate that Rwanda was the most Christian nation in Africa, with over 90 percent of Rwandans having been baptized as Christians. Yet, over the course of just a few months, this very "reached" nation committed one of the most horrendous acts ever committed by humanity. Paul Washer wrote, "We are not only called to proclaim truth . . . we must also explain to them what they must do. Proclamations and the words that form them are important, but only to the degree that they are properly defined and applied. Such is the case of the Gospel."[5]

Missionaries must know not only what to teach but also what not to teach. It is essential to teach the whole counsel of the Word of God and basic theology, and then assist in the application of these truths in the cultural context. Themes and topics pertinent to one culture may need more or less depth of treatment in another. For instance, systematic theologies developed in the West rarely delve deeply into the reasons for, and cultural consequences of, polygamy and animism.

Since ecclesiology drives missiology, a crucial question must be addressed: What is a church? Obviously, the space in this chapter does not allow a profound treatment. However, some very basic guidelines provide a sufficient description for the depth we need here. Historically, the marks of a true church are preaching of the Word, observance of the ordinances of Lord's Supper and baptism, and church discipline. The International Mission Board of the Southern Baptist Convention has adopted a definition that is more than adequate for their missionary members to recognize a New Testament church (see Appendix). The definition is biblical and covers a number of detailed aspects of the local church such as preeminence of the Word of God, ordinances, and leadership. While your church may not adhere to this exact definition, any biblical study seeking to define a New Testament church reveals that it is not simply a group of people who have decided to meet and read the Bible together. It is important that missionaries teach nationals what the Bible says about the church and not leave them to define it for themselves based purely on preference for existing cultural forms or what might be the most expedient.

Pastor Mark Dever has helped pastors and elders to understand the marks of a healthy church. Each of the nine marks that Dever delineates flows into the next, forming a logical conclusion from the previous one that also points to the next. He has written extensively that a healthy church should be characterized by expository preaching, biblical theology, a biblical understanding of the gospel, a biblical understanding of conversion, biblical evangelism, a biblical understanding of church membership, biblical church discipline, biblical discipleship and Christian growth in the church, and biblical church leadership. To be sure, Dever is not saying that these are the essential requirements for a group to be a true church; rather, these are the marks of one that is healthy. When missionaries instruct national pastors in the marks of a true church as well as these biblical guidelines for *healthy* churches, the result will be sound, reproducing, and enduring testimonies of the power of God in the cultures of the world.

There are many aspects of biblical and theological truth to teach in pastoral preparation, leadership training, and theological education. All of them must contextualize and communicate the message in culturally appropriate forms. Teaching the head is only one aspect of biblical leadership training.

The Hands

The ministry force must receive more than a mere transfer of knowledge from one brain to another; there must also be a skill set developed in the lives and ministries of the leaders. Some training programs refer to this as practical theology. Since missionaries received their training in practical theology in Western systems, they often have to rethink how this information will find expression in the new culture. For instance, the deductive reasoning and three points utilized in many Western pulpits is illogical and unintelligible to the minds of many in other cultures. A story, metaphor, parable, or extended illustration, such as we see in the teaching ministry of Jesus, is more understandable to many non-Western hearers. Therefore, the preaching style that missionaries utilize may need to be decidedly different.

Even aspects of the missionary task as universal as sharing the gospel must take cultural and worldview distinctions into account. Witnessing in the West has traditionally revolved around a shared Judeo-Christian worldview. Virtually all evangelistic programs assume that the presenter and the hearer share the same modern worldview. More than one evangelistic method includes the use of diagnostic questions such as, "Have you come to the place in your life where you know for certain if you died today that you would go to heaven?" Or, "Suppose you were standing before God and He should ask you, Why should I let you into My heaven? What do you think you would say?" Both of these questions presuppose that the hearer believes in the God of the Bible, heaven and hell, sin, etc. Many other cultures have worldviews that would preclude the use of such witnessing tools. The key to effective evangelism is not the mastery of an evangelistic method from your home culture; it is knowing Jesus Christ, His Word, and the target culture so well that you can share the gospel without a memorized pre-packaged approach.

I HAVE SEEN THAT who teaches the theology in a seminary influences the minds of future leaders and who teaches the courses on evangelism and church growth influences the feet of the students.

—DAVID BLEDSOE

Urban evangelist and church planting trainer,
Brazil

A more complex challenge is the fact that many national leaders in countries around the world received their Bible college or seminary education from Western missionaries who never considered any cultural differences beyond the language barrier. The Western professor-missionaries simply translated their notes and taught the national pastors exactly what they learned when they were in school in the USA. The order in which they presented topics of instruction, the delivery system, lecture style, dress, classroom arrangement, teaching techniques such as book reviews, lectures, and research papers were all mirrored reflections of their seminary days—only in a different language. When newer missionaries seek to prepare national leaders using more culturally appropriate teaching models and techniques, they often encounter opposition from missionaries—

as well as national pastors trained in the old system. The new methods may seem to them to be "dumbing down" the necessary instruction. It is no wonder that many missionaries opt out of training nationals completely when it seems the only other option is to train them in culturally inappropriate ways that cannot be perpetuated by the nationals in future ministry. This concept of contextualization is covered in more depth in chapter 10.

National pastors must learn to pastor, preach, teach, counsel, evangelize, lead Bible studies, and practice personal spiritual disciplines at the very least. Donald McGavran emphasized that the biblical pattern is for missionaries to identify and train national leaders. McGavran wrote, "Paul was the first leader of the churches in Galatia and boldly claimed that they were his children, that he was 'in travail' with them over and over again until they should be formed in Christ (Galatians 4:19). But like Paul, as soon as possible the missionaries discover and train indigenous leaders from among the tribesmen and women themselves."[6] The hands in the ministry must learn how to teach others to teach others. Only in this way will sound ministry practices continue.

The Heart

Character issues in leaders have often been overlooked in many pastoral preparation and leadership training programs. Those preparing new generations of ministers and leaders should not assume the presence of these characteristics in the lives of young leaders, nor should they assume that that they will automatically appear upon instruction in other areas. While only the Lord can look on the heart, those involved in leadership training should seek to ensure that those they are training and recommending meet the qualifications of leaders with hearts after God's own heart. Many rapid-multiplication church planting efforts do not see intentional church leadership as necessary, and if they have leadership at all, biblical qualifications are rarely addressed. For example, even in denominations that insist pastors and elders be only men, many of the churches planted in their name and at their expense have women pastors. One missionary operating under this principle explained that he gets around this by not calling the women pastors, even though they function as pastors and consider themselves to be so. One missionary to China reveals that 80 percent of the house church pastors are women. It is incredibly hard to inculcate a sense of integrity in the ministries of church leaders when some of their missionaries fail to model it themselves.

WHAT SHOULD NEW BELIEVERS know before they are qualified to lead? In the past, missionaries waited decades before giving believers leadership responsibility. Today, some church planting models insist on giving brand new believers pastoral roles prior to any theological training. The Bible opts for a balance somewhere between these two extremes. Trusted new believers in the nascent church should be encouraged to take leadership roles commensurate with growing maturity and ability. For leaders who seek to become pastors of local churches, however, the pathway to this position must follow the clear signposts of the Word. Paul waited until his second visit to appoint leaders in the first new churches (Acts 13–14), even though these Jewish Christians had received scriptural training in the synagogues. Further, Paul tells Timothy that he is not to place novices (1 Timothy 3:6) into pastoral roles; in fact, Timothy himself (a missionary) is commanded to train leaders in the context of the local assembly (2 Timothy 2:2). This training involves a specific body of knowledge ("what you have heard from me") that current leaders must entrust to each generation. There is no shortcut.

—STAN MAY

Chairman & Professor of Missions,
Mid-America Baptist Theological Seminary
Former Missionary to Zimbabwe

The Bible speaks very plainly about the qualifications of pastors and leaders. In 1 Timothy 3 and Titus 1, Paul gives instructions about the kind of men who should be pastors. He mentions requirements such as above reproach, husband of one wife, sober-minded, disciplined, self-controlled, respectable, hospitable, able to teach, not a drunkard, not violent but gentle, not arrogant or quick-tempered, not a lover of money, God's steward, keeps his children submissive, not a recent convert, well thought of by outsiders, a lover of good, upright, and holy. The pastoral office is not the only role with specific biblical qualifications. First Timothy 3 provides the qualifications and required characteristics of deacons: dignified, not double-tongued, not addicted to much wine, not greedy for dishonest gain, clear conscience, tested, blameless, husband of one wife, and one who manages his children and household well. Clearly, a man who meets these qualifications would provide the kind of leadership that the fledgling churches would need to grow in godliness. It is noteworthy that Paul does not only say "able to teach" as a requirement to be pastor or elder; he lists all of those other characteristics as well. In other words, theological education is only one aspect of the qualifications. However, it is also significant to note that he does not leave "able to teach" out. Being able to teach is an essential requirement of biblical church leadership. Yet, being able to teach requires having a credible testimony of faithfulness and honesty as well as knowing the truth. The head, hands, and heart are all important in a biblically qualified leader.

Rapid church multiplication models often insist on lay leadership because training pastors takes time and slows down the multiplication process. Since the Bible is not clear regarding ordination matters, the use of lay leaders is perfectly fine—as long as they are biblically qualified and trained. While every church member should be able to function as a minister to those around him or her, we must never belittle the role or the value of a qualified, trained pastor.

The belief that church leadership is not necessary—or is even detrimental—to healthy church growth is entirely without biblical justification and in direct opposition to both scriptural guidelines and apostolic practice. To be fair, many insist upon unpaid and untrained lay ministers only when "no formal seminaries are available, formal education requirements would limit the pool of potential leaders, 'extras' would slow down preparation time, and salaries would slow down the multiplication of churches."[7] However, would there ever be a time when this is not the case? This logic flows out of the need for speed. Speeding the multiplication of church plants means jettisoning that which slows it down. What is so dangerous here is that they jettison biblical requirements for the sake of expediency. The hearts of the pastors and national leaders should be characterized by love— love for God, love for His Word, love for the world, and love for individuals. This love will spur them on to spend and be spent to get the training necessary for the ministry God has called them to do in a way that not only advances the kingdom but also glorifies Him. Their hearts are also to be filled with love for the church. This love motivates them to plant and develop healthy churches that are grounded in the truth. As my alma mater describes its ministry, so these pastors could be described: A mind for truth, a heart for God.

Living It Out

While working among indigenous peoples in the Andes, I often taught basic Bible doctrines to national pastors, leaders, and churches using several methods for teaching that did not require seminaries, libraries, or computers. These methods are as simple as the teachers who employed them, but they resulted in trained leadership among indigenous national believers. Saturday workshops in tiny Andean churches, in the yard outside indigenous homes, and in cinder-block church buildings in the poorer areas of Quito became our training schools where I taught believers to understand and apply the Word of God.

We utilized a children's catechism, and we told Bible stories chronologically to develop an overview of the Bible among the national people. Additionally, I used a very basic systematic theology outline to teach them doctrine. It was little more than the headings one would expect to find in a systematic theology text, with a couple of explanatory paragraphs and biblical citations under each heading. In addition to providing an outline for ready reference in the weekly teaching sessions, it ensured that no essential doctrine would be overlooked.

CONCLUSION

Preparation is not only imparting knowledge, it is also training trainers to ensure that those who follow are ready, willing, and able to continue the process. As pastors and leaders learn, they are preparing their minds. As they minister, they are preparing their hands. And as they serve in love, they are preparing their hearts. Paul Washer reminds us that the more one learns about God and His Word, the more one is compelled to serve in faithfulness. "We have forgotten that genuine, enduring passion is born out of one's knowledge of the truth, and specifically the truth of the Gospel. The more one comprehends its beauty, the more one will be apprehended by its power."[8]

As in many aspects of life, these pastors will learn best by doing. In the same way that students of other disciplines may spend many hours merely reading or studying about their work, the day eventually comes when they must practice it. The pilot must leave ground school to get in the plane and actually fly, the pianist must actually play the piano, the swimmer must get in the pool, and the bicycle rider must ride if he is truly to learn. Mentoring mentors, in actual practice, is simply the ancient and biblical model of master and apprentice.

One of the best video presentations of this model in practice is the classic, *EE-taow!*, and its follow-up, *The Next Chapter*. In these two videos, Mark Zook presents the gospel to the Mouk tribe in Papua New Guinea by telling Bible stories. After the tribe comes to Christ, Mark challenges them to take the message to other tribes, using the same methodology. Because Mark had used a reproducible model, they were able to use it to share the gospel with others. In the next village, Mark repeated his stories while the Mouk believers watched and assisted him. At the next village, the Mouk believers told the stories, and Mark watched and assisted them. In the subsequent villages, the ministry was completely in Mouk hands. Preliterate tribal people were teaching the truth to other preliterate tribal people in biblically responsible, culturally appropriate ways.

The bare minimum that missionaries should teach must result in trained leadership in the national church that is able to interpret the Word of God (2 Timothy 2:15), understand basic Christian doctrines (1 Timothy 4:6), and teach them to others (1 Timothy 3:2). They must also meet the biblical qualifications of church leaders (1 Timothy 3:1–7) and know how to critically contextualize the gospel in their culture (1 Corinthians 9:22). Furthermore, they should have a general background of the history of Christianity so that with the knowledge of the errors and victories of the past they can stand on the shoulders of those who have gone before and see farther down the road than their forebears could. They must also be equipped in wise practices for church polity, administration, and practical ministry skills. How much is enough? They must be able to teach the Scriptures, sound doctrine, and godly living to those who follow; less than that is not enough.

Suggested Reading

Adam, Peter. "Preaching and Biblical Theology." In *New Dictionary of Biblical Theology: Exploring the Unity & Diversity of Scripture*, edited by Brian S. Rosner, T. Desmond Alexander, Graeme Goldsworthy, and D. A. Carson, 104–12. Downers Grove, IL: InterVarsity Press, 2000.

Engel, James F. "Beyond the Numbers Game," *Christianity Today*, August 7, 2000.

McGavran, Donald. *Ethnic Realities and the Church: Lessons from India*. Pasadena, CA: William Carey Library, 1979.

Mock, Dennis J. "Course Manuals 1-10." Bible Training Centre for Pastors and Church Leaders, 1989.

Sanders, J. Oswald. *Spiritual Discipleship: Principles of Following Christ for Every Believer.* Chicago: Moody Publishers, 2007.

_____. *Spiritual Leadership: Principles of Excellence for Every Believer.* Chicago: Moody Publishers, 2007.

_____. *Spiritual Maturity: Principles of Spiritual Growth for Every Believer.* Chicago: Moody Publishers, 2007.

Sproul, R. C. *Essential Truths of the Christian Faith.* Chicago: Tyndale, 1998.

Washer, Paul. "Gospel 101," *HeartCry* Magazine 54 (September–November 2007): 1–6.

4

MISSIONARIES AND NATIONALS: WHO SHOULD TEACH?

Thus far the argument may appear overwhelming that the missionaries should be the teachers. The problems that develop when missionaries do not teach long enough or broadly enough are obvious. One could argue that the missionaries should be the teachers because they have the training. However, there is also a strong argument that the nationals would be the better teachers for their own people. After all, the nationals have the language and culture, which renders them better equipped for the task of training in many respects. There are other reasons why the Western missionary may not be the best choice for teaching others.

Often missionaries cannot obtain visas that allow open Christian ministry in the countries they serve. Missiologists refer to these places as creative access countries because the missionaries who serve there must find "creative" reasons for the governments to let them in. Often, the missionary teaches English as a Second Language or works as a business consultant to obtain a visa. However, Western missions need to learn that creative access does not always have to refer to the missionaries themselves gaining access to closed countries. It could very well be that the best and most creative access would be equipping and enabling nationals to do ministry there. Even in the case of unreached areas where there are no converts to train, Western missionaries could educate and train believers from other countries, who do not have USA passports, to serve as theological educators and pastoral trainers. Missionaries in neighboring countries or near-culture areas could train pastors and professors and send them as a teaching force into yet unreached areas of the world. Westerners could creatively access ministry opportunities in these countries by using their education, training, expertise, and funds to develop a cadre of trained trainers for believers in national churches around world. The challenge of creative access countries does not preclude fulfilling the biblical commands to teach them to observe everything Christ commanded us.

The question of whether missionaries or nationals should be the teachers does not demand an either/or answer as if the two options are mutually exclusive. For instance, one ministry promotes the idea of supporting national missionaries in addition to its use of Westerners and defends its use of both. Paul Washer's ministry perspective is that "although HeartCry recognizes the great importance of sending missionaries from the West to the unevangelized peoples throughout the world, we believe that we are led of the Lord to support indigenous or native missionaries so that they might evangelize their own peoples. We seek to work with indigenous congregations, elders, and missionaries of integrity and faith in the unreached world to help them evangelize and plant churches among their own peoples."[1]

Washer continues by explaining that his ministry's philosophy includes theological education. "HeartCry will seek to contribute to the continued theological and ministerial training of the missionaries it sponsors. This will be accomplished through such things as Bible conferences, literature distribution, and theological training by extension."[2] This perspective for using national and Western missionaries is valid for employing both as professors in theological education as well.

We would do well to remember that behind everything is the gifting and guiding of the Holy Spirit. We should not seek to defend our placement of personnel in the places and ministries they serve as if we were the ones who make all the decisions. God is the one who gifts missionaries and guides them to the places of service that He has for them (Acts 17:26; Ephesians 2:10). Every believer should be aware of individual gifts and seek to develop them. Moreover, knowing one's passion area for using spiritual gifts is the path to joyful, fruitful edification of the body of Christ. Indeed, in local churches a congregation is blessed when her members not only know their spiritual gifts and passion areas for using them, but also have the freedom to minister with them in that local body. In the same way, missionaries should have opportunities to serve as professors preparing national leaders when God has gifted, educated, and called them to do so. Likewise, gifted and educated national brothers whom God has called to teach should seek and find available to them the places of service that He desires (Ecclesiastes 9:10; Ephesians 4:11–14).

NATIONALS AS TEACHERS

Nationals can do evangelism and discipleship in culturally appropriate ways better than Westerners can. However, very often their service is not appreciated or utilized. The problem is not one of ability; many countries have trained national brothers who have no educational ministry opportunities. Many seminary graduates among the national brothers do not find acceptance in the Western-model educational institutions in their countries because their own national brothers do not view them as sufficiently knowledgeable in comparison to the Western M.Div. and Ph.D. degreed professors. The thinking that only a graduate of a USA-based theological seminary is qualified to teach pastors is unfortunately commonplace, but it is absolutely unfounded and unbiblical. Paul Washer writes about the value of the national brothers' ministries, "As a result of two millennia of cross-cultural missionary work, there are untold millions of Christians throughout the world. Dedicated to God, knowledgeable of the Scriptures, and with a burning zeal for the lost, they often suffer great hardship, risking life and personal welfare to preach the Gospel to their own people. The indigenous or native missionary strategy recognizes the worth and usefulness of this great body of native believers and seeks to provide the training and financial support necessary for them to reach their own people."[3]

WITH MORE THAN TWENTY years of experience in training youth workers internationally, I am convinced that the primary duty of missions is to train national leaders for the work of implementing and leading the work of the local church. Further, we should place a priority of effort on "training the trainers" of national workers. We in evangelical missions have learned well the work of "addition" missions (evangelism and church planting), but we have failed to learn the lesson of "multiplication" missions (equipping national leadership). Multiplication missions work is that which is dedicated to the reaching and teaching of national leaders with the ultimate goal of preparing them to not only do the work of the ministry without dependency on the missionary (Ephesians 4:11–13), but to also be able as qualified leaders to teach and train other national workers at the highest spiritual, practical, and theological level (2 Timothy 2:2).

—RANDY SMITH

Assistant Professor of Youth Ministry,
Boyce College
Associate Director, International Center
for Youth Ministry

Many missionaries have often tried to excuse themselves from service because of the language barrier and the fear that they just cannot learn another language. Nevertheless, after a couple of years struggling to learn the language, developing sermons, writing lesson plans, and preparing to preach and teach in the language, they find themselves in the seminary classroom. However, the true difficulty of the language barrier is that it is not restricted to the vocabulary and grammar, but includes all the idioms, dialects, and pronunciation as well. Compounding the challenge is the fact that many seminary classrooms will have several dialects represented. Indeed, some seminaries are regional training institutions with students from many countries, a dynamic that further complicates communication. All of the twenty-two countries in which Spanish is the primary language count numerous dialects and accents within them, and some accents are virtually unintelligible to a foreigner who has learned another. Common vocabulary in one country will be offensive in another. Sometimes the words are not interchangeable at all. For instance, the word *huahua* means "bus" in Cuba, but "baby" in Ecuador. This challenge would be difficult for anyone, but it is almost insurmountable for a foreign missionary who has a low level of language skills. Nationals are the best teachers and facilitators in such multicultural classrooms.

National professors also share the worldview and culture of the students. Knowledge of the culture, customs, legends, and myths in the culture equips them with an endless supply of illustrations when teaching. This knowledge also arms them with the essential background to avoid syncretism in teaching and to recognize it when it creeps in among the students. A thorough grounding in traditions, old wives' tales, gender roles, and appropriate humor are aspects of the culture that take missionaries many years to learn—if they ever do. Professors from within the culture will be able to utilize these aspects in their teaching to contextualize the information in the culture in ways that the students will recognize, embrace, and assimilate from the very beginning.

I was once teaching a group of Quichua leaders in a drafty hut at twelve thousand feet above sea level, and it was very cold. One of them was sick with a cold when he arrived and he generously passed it around, so as the week continued there was a lot of sneezing. I always said, "God bless you," after each sneeze. This brought on uncontrollable giggles every time it happened. After a couple of days, my curiosity got the best of me, and I stopped my teaching to ask what was so funny. They hesitantly informed me that the joke in their culture was that when someone sneezed, he was thinking about his mistress. Of course, these men did not have mistresses, but my remark made it appear to them that I thought they did, and was asking God to bless them when they thought about her. This was not a major cultural incident, and it was soon understood and overcome. However, in the back of my mind I wondered how much of my teaching in that intensive week of classes they had missed because of their giggling about my cultural misunderstanding.

The greatest advantage that a national professor brings to the table is his awareness of the culture that enables him to avoid syncretism. Syncretism is almost impossible to avoid and will almost always occur at some level. However, as Paul Hiebert points out so clearly, the failure to understand the folk religions that exist when one is evangelizing or teaching will virtually guarantee that syncretism will result.[4] Old religions do not go away when people embrace new ones—even Christianity. They go underground and are always looking for an opportunity to pop back out. Professors from within the culture who have come out of traditional religious backgrounds are able to guard against the insidious creep of syncretism in a way that outsiders never can.

Another reason for training and embracing national brothers as professors is because the task is both great and growing. As the number of believers grows, the missionaries are increasingly overwhelmed as they seek to disciple, train, and teach them. Some have inexplicably argued that when the growth of the church is more than missionaries can manage, this is reason enough not to train. Hoyt Lovelace responds, "When there is a greater supply of new converts, they demand a greater supply of trainers and assistants."[5] Donald McGavran concurs:

Missionaries are an essential part of the spread of the Gospel and give birth to new churches. Like all good mothers they nurse their children and direct their ways. In the beginning, they have to be quite visible, transmitting the faith, translating the Bible, establishing new habits of worship and behavior, discouraging lying, hatred, and sexual sins, and encouraging mutual respect, love, and forgiveness of enemies. Having travailed, given birth, and cared for young churches, the missionaries (whether Tamilian or Naga or American or Australian) should turn over authority to indigenous leaders. These must be discovered, trained, and installed in their tribes.[6]

These national brothers are very often sincere and committed men who simply lack training. Indeed, many of these men will suffer in ways and sacrifice in places that some missionaries will not. Paul Washer writes, "In my ten years as a missionary in Peru, I met indigenous missionaries of whom the world is not worthy. These are men who would stand for hours and preach while being mocked and beaten and having goat urine poured on their heads. They would preach until their persecutors grew tired, sat down, and listened! I know men who look like toothless, sandal-footed beggars, and yet they have started ten or fifteen churches."[7]

WESTERN MISSIONARIES AS TEACHERS

Missionaries who have spent years studying the Scriptures in doctrinally sound theological seminaries bring not only their own lives and teaching skills to invest in the preparation of nationals, they also bring over two thousand years of theological reflection that was part of their training. Such depth and background enables them to shed light on God's Word in ways that are not innate or automatic in Christian experience. All the learning that missionaries have received renders them able teachers. The calling they have received to be missionary-professors equips them with gifts, passion, and joy in that ministry. When a people group first accepts the gospel, they obviously need sound teachers to instruct them in the Word. Additionally, many cultures that have had churches for years may still need teachers from the outside since no one has ever taught them or trained teachers among them.

I BELIEVE WE HAVE been romantic in our view of working ourselves out of a job in the area of training and teaching the nationals and that this has been our detriment in the historic mission fields. I believe in the principles of self-governing, self-sustaining, and self-propagating; however, this is more for the local church and not as cleanly applicable to a nation, a people group, and an association of churches that need specialized assistance in teaching and theological education.

—DAVID BLEDSOE

Urban Evangelist and Church
Planting Trainer, Brazil

Even though doctrinally sound Western missionaries are necessary until teachers have been prepared within the culture, they must be careful that they do not unwittingly bring negative aspects from their home church cultures. Some missionaries come from traditions with extrabiblical definitions of sin, such as not going to movies, not dancing, or not playing card games. When they export these definitions of sin without a thorough explanation as to why they believe they are sinful—which they may not even know themselves—they often inculcate a tendency toward legalism. They may also bring error when they have not been adequately trained in sound theology themselves. David Bledsoe writes of the country where he serves, "Missionaries by and large serve in roles that give them an ability to influence national leadership, especially the upcoming generation. This inspiration can be positive or negative, constructive or destructive. Although the examples are few, some professor-missionaries transmitted liberal theological tenets to past and present-day evangelical leaders."[8] Arguments could be set forth for and against the use of both missionary outsiders and national insiders in training and education, but what does our authoritative source say?

THE BIBLE WEIGHS IN

A number of biblical passages teach very clearly that the ones with knowledge are to teach those who come after them. The Bible does not present the duty to teach them as an optional assignment if one has time or happens to be so inclined. If the Bible is our only rule of faith and practice, missionaries should look to it and follow it in all that it teaches. Let us consider a few passages to see the mind of God in this matter.

Genesis 18:19 teaches, "For I have chosen him, that he may command his children and his household after him to keep the way of the Lord by doing righteousness and justice, so that the Lord may bring to Abraham what he has promised him."

Deuteronomy 4:9 teaches the Israelites, "Only take care, and keep your soul diligently, lest you forget the things that your eyes have seen, and lest they depart from your heart all the days of your life. Make them known to your children and your children's children."

Deuteronomy 6:1–6 teaches, "Now this is the commandment, the statutes and the rules that the Lord your God commanded me to teach you, that you may do them in the land to which you are going over, to possess it, that you may fear the Lord your God, you and your son and your son's son, by keeping all his statutes and his commandments, which I command you, all the days of your life, and that your days may be long. Hear therefore, O Israel, and be careful to do them, that it may go well with you, and that you may multiply greatly, as the Lord, the God of your fathers, has promised you, in a land flowing with milk and honey. Hear, O Israel: The Lord our God, the Lord is one. You shall love the Lord your God with all your heart and with all your soul and with all your might. And these words that I command you today shall be on your heart."

Deuteronomy 11:19 teaches, "You shall teach them to your children, talking of them when you are sitting in your house, and when you are walking by the way, and when you lie down, and when you rise."

Deuteronomy 32:46 teaches, "Take to heart all the words by which I am warning you today, that you may command them to your children, that they may be careful to do all the words of this law."

Psalm 78:4–6 teaches, "We will not hide them from their children, but tell to the coming generation the glorious deeds of the Lord, and his might, and the wonders that he has done. He established a testimony in Jacob and appointed a law in Israel, which he commanded our fathers to teach to their children, that the next generation might know them, the children yet unborn, and arise and tell them to their children."

Clearly, these passages represent the command of God that those who know should teach those who come behind them who do not yet know, so that they may teach the ones who will follow them. In each case, the Bible is telling the hearers to teach their children. Two truths stand out. One is that in order for men and women to teach their children, they must know the truth profoundly themselves. However, someone may point out that these passages refer to teaching our children, not to teaching in general. Therefore, the second truth is that we must never forget that those who follow us in the faith are our spiritual children (1 Corinthians 4:17; 1 Timothy 1:2; Titus 1:4; Philemon 10). Obviously, those who have the knowledge— i.e., the missionaries and evangelists—should be the initial teachers. However, they should be zealous and proactive to prepare the nationals to assume the role of teacher, professor, and pastor as the Holy Spirit calls them.

The lives of the nationals and those who learn from them are blessed when they faithfully and correctly fulfill their ministries. Ezra 7:9–10 teaches us that God's enabling hand and His blessing was on Ezra because he was faithful to study God's Word, sought to live it out, and faithfully taught it to others. For the national brothers to study it, practice it themselves, and teach it to others, we must first teach them, and then we must empower them to continue the work of teaching others.

Matthew 28:18–20 contains Jesus' last command to His followers prior to His ascension. "And Jesus came and said to them, 'All authority in heaven and on earth has been given to me. Go therefore and make disciples of all nations, baptizing them in the name of the Father and of the Son and of the Holy Spirit, teaching them to observe all that I have commanded you. And behold, I am with you always, to the end of the age.'" Jesus not only commands His followers to make disciples, He tells them how to do this—preaching the Word, baptizing them, and teaching them to observe/obey *all* He has commanded us. Only those who have this body of knowledge may pass it on. It falls to missionaries to prepare their hearers in this way if they are to be faithful to the Lord's command.

Paul provides clear biblical guidance for missionary activity in 2 Timothy 2:2, "And what you have heard from me in the presence of many witnesses entrust to faithful men who will be able to teach others also." Only in this way will future generations have sound teachers, biblical doctrine, and the pure gospel as those before them received it. Those who have the truth must faithfully teach it to those who follow. Paul goes on to teach that merely having a Bible is not sufficient. We must teach those we reach to interpret it correctly in order for them to receive the benefits that Paul's writings promise and to be equipped for useful service. In 2 Timothy 3:16–17, Paul writes, "All Scripture is breathed out by God and profitable for teaching, for reproof, for correction, and for training in righteousness, that the man of God may be competent, equipped for every good work." The duty to teach and train those who come behind is inescapable; God's Word does not allow for any other path if the missionary wants to be faithful in discharging his duty. In addition, in the apostle John's gospel we find the teaching from the Lord Jesus to all who follow Him, "If you love me, you will keep my commandments" (John 14:15).

LANGUAGE AND CULTURAL CONSIDERATIONS

Evangelical leaders among Highland Quichuas in the Andes revealed that their greatest need was trained leadership for the churches. I knew that the only existing training and education programs in the country were for the dominant culture and were in Spanish. Throughout the region, Quichuas are approximately 80 to 85 percent monolingual in Quichua, with the majority of the bilingual people being children or juveniles. When I asked the leaders what language we should use for the training, they responded, "Both Spanish and Quichua." They explained that the Quichua language did not have all of the necessary theological and biblical terms, and that Spanish words would have to be borrowed to teach some ideas and concepts. However, they insisted that we also retain Quichua because most of those who would be the age of pastoral authority did not speak Spanish.

Historically, missionaries who are training nationals will choose the path of least resistance. If the missionary only speaks the language of the dominant culture, he must teach through an interpreter or only accept bilinguals into the program. The latter option is the most common since the library already contains books that the bilingual will be able to read for study in the seminary. When a missionary-professor has access to multiple resources such as Bibles, commentaries, theology books, developed arguments, and a theological vocabulary, it takes an overwhelming reason to the contrary for him not to use them and require the learner to adapt to the dominant culture's language. However, missionaries must remember that those who wrote those resources came from a worldview that is completely foreign to the people group he is trying to teach.

During his early missions experience as a colporteur, Cam Townsend, founder of Wycliffe Bible Translators, encountered many indigenous groups in Mexico and Guatemala who could neither communicate in nor read Spanish. He came to see the value of communicating the gospel to people in their heart language (or mother tongue). Donald McGavran also found that people hear the gospel and worship best when they do not have to cross barriers to do so. McGavran developed this initial observation into the Homogeneous Unit Principle during his years of serving in India among people divided by three thousand castes of Hinduism. National professors have cultural skills that they bring to the training system that the Western missionary does not possess, and the Western missionary often brings sound theology and biblical knowledge that the national professor may not yet have.

I THINK THAT THE TEACHERS should ideally be members of the culture itself. This assumes they have had training, and perhaps supervision, from thoroughly trained missionaries who understand cultural anthropology. Unfortunately, today we frequently have missionaries in Latin America coming from the United States with little or no training of any kind. On the other hand, Latin American missionaries are trying not to repeat the same negative cultural model that we received in the past, while still trying to leave space for leaders from the local culture. Ultimately, one should teach that it is the culture that should be adjusted to the gospel and not the other way around.

—JOSELITO ORELLANA
Missionary, Ecuador
President, Ecuadorian Baptist
Theological Seminary

It was obvious when training the Quichua people that both languages were necessary in the instruction, and, as soon as possible, they needed teachers from both cultures. Westerners are needed to teach pastors with the vast resources of their training, and national professors are needed to ensure that they learn it in purity without unintended cultural baggage or syncretism. Additionally, employing trained teachers from both cultures promotes unity and the family bond that believers share. McGavran wrote, "All types of Churches constantly stress brotherhood, equality, fellowship, and justice. They do this because the Bible and the Holy Spirit require it. Theological training at all levels builds brotherhood. Literature builds brotherhood. The international Church insists on it. There is an irreversible trend to brotherhood."[9] Paul Washer argues the need for both outsiders and nationals to serve together, even as he makes a strong appeal to support indigenous workers. "The indigenous missionary strategy does not eliminate the need for cross-cultural missionaries. This is not an either/or, but a both/and situation. We are not arguing for a moratorium on North American and Western European missionaries, but fully recognize the need for thousands more on the field! We are simply seeking to prove that the indigenous missionary strategy is an equally viable, and in some cases, more effective missionary method."[10]

Teaching Styles

Virtually every Western teaching method and training program incorporates components that are foreign to most other cultures. The exceptions are the countries that Westerners colonized in the past or have heavily influenced in this age of globalization. Components that are common to Western education programs include classrooms with desks, teachers lecturing to note-takers, a heavy emphasis on clock time, and linear sequential logic. Virtually all of these components are polar opposites of the cultural traditional training models around the world. One aspect of Western education that the missionary may not even be aware of is the hidden curriculum. Judith Lingenfelter explains that Western education teaches turn-taking, respect for elders, being polite, standing in line, respecting the personal space and rights of others, and the value of honesty in our education models from kindergarten onward.[11] Of course, this information is not explicitly taught in textbooks or lectures; it is hidden in the subtle ways in which one learns within the system. Missionary-professors often expect nationals to already possess this "education" and are surprised to find that even adult students lack it.

Additionally, Western missionaries are largely unaware of their own ethnocentric tendencies and preferences, especially regarding what they consider to be the best teaching methods. James W. Stigler and James Hiebert write, "Teaching is a cultural activity. We learn how to teach indirectly, through years of participation in classroom life, and we are largely unaware of some of the most widespread attributes of teaching in our own culture. . . . The fact that teaching is a cultural activity explains why teaching has been so resistant to change. But recognizing the cultural nature of teaching gives us new insights into what we need to do if we wish to improve it."[12] National teachers will be able to teach in culturally appropriate ways as a matter of second nature, whereas Western missionaries must labor to understand the cultures and languages. Again, Stigler and Hiebert state, "Cultural activities, such as teaching, are not invented full-blown but rather evolve over long periods of time in ways that are consistent with the stable web of beliefs and assumptions that are part of the culture."[13] This supports the position that national professors should be equipped and entrusted with the work of training instead of building training programs on the foundation of Western models that depend on the presence of Western professors. "Cultural activities are highly stable over time, and they are not easily changed. This is true for two reasons. First, cultural activities are systems, and systems—especially complex ones, such as teaching—can be very difficult to change. The second reason is that cultural activities are embedded in a wider culture, often in ways not readily apparent to members of the culture. If we want to improve teaching, both its systemic and its cultural aspects must be recognized and addressed."[14]

The educational models in the Global South's face-to-face cultures are characterized by mentoring, master/apprentice, and watch-and-do methods. This is especially true when teaching gender-specific roles such as sowing, cultivating, harvesting, animal husbandry, and house-building skills to boys, or child-rearing, home-care, and cooking skills to girls. There are no classes for these learning activities;

they simply watch and do. It is very common to see young indigenous girls with a doll, lamb, or puppy tied in a shawl on their backs,
just as they have seen their own mothers carrying their little brothers and sisters. The countless differences between majority world
cultures in the Global South as opposed to the technologically developed West are often stormy seas for foreign missionary-professors to
navigate that would be smooth sailing for a national professor.

There are many other arguments for including both Western-
trained missionaries and national professors in the faculty. While the
national professor may have the linguistic and cultural skills that are
invaluable in the educational institution, the advanced degrees of
the Western missionary may be more attractive to the pertinent
accreditation agency. In some countries, the government acts in this
capacity and demands that all institutions of higher education only
employ faculty that hold terminal degrees. In other cases, professors
are required to have a degree that is at least one degree higher than
the level he or she teaches in the country. For instance, a master's
degree is necessary to teach at the bachelor's level and a doctoral
degree is required to teach at the master's level. In such cases, the
seminary must reduce its degree offerings significantly or close completely if the Western missionary leaves.

CONCLUSION

The missionary must be the first teacher; he alone has the knowledge in the beginning that must be learned by the rest, and he serves
as a pastor/guide/mentor. However, he should also begin with the
understanding that he is not just teaching students or preparing pastors; he should aim to teach teachers and train trainers. His role will
change through time as the national leaders are equipped to carry on
the work with his direct daily involvement. This role adjustment
should occur naturally as the national leaders' knowledge grows and
their abilities mature, much as a father will naturally adjust his level
of involvement as his child grows into adulthood. As nationals are
discipled and trained, their cultural knowledge and background will

enhance the teaching of other nationals, but this does not necessarily mean that the Western missionary must move on. A father may pass his knowledge and even the legal ownership of the family business to a son and continue to work with his son for the rest of his life. The son will assume more and more direction, but a godly, balanced dad will always be ready to step in and offer wise counsel when needed and requested. In the same way, missionaries should educate national brothers with the goal of welcoming them into the work of training others. Missionaries and nationals each bring unique gifts and skills to the essential work of preparing leadership, "Teaching everyone with all wisdom, that we may present everyone mature in Christ" (Colossians 1:28).

Suggested Reading

Brynjolfson, Robert and Jonathan Lewis, eds. *Integral Ministry Training: Design and Evaluation.* Pasadena, CA: William Carey Library, 2006.

Lingenfelter, Judith E. and Sherwood G. *Teaching Cross-Culturally: An Incarnational Model for Learning and Teaching.* Grand Rapids: Baker Academic, 2003.

Stigler, James W. and James Hiebert. *The Teaching Gap.* New York: Simon & Schuster, 1999.

Washer, Paul. "Indigenous Missions." *HeartCry* Magazine 56 (February 2008): 16–23.

LEARNING FROM PAUL: MISSIOLOGICAL METHODS OF THE APOSTLE TO THE GENTILES

The focal point of this examination of the task of international missions is whether missionaries should primarily reach and leave or reach and teach. Consider the question in the light of what God Himself calls missionaries to do. In *The Missionary Call*, I reported how the church has historically viewed the missionary call. There have been numerous positions through the years, but they tend to fall into one of three basic categories.

MISSIONARY CALLINGS

One view of the missionary call is that there is no call. The Bible does not say in Ephesians 4:11, "And he gave the apostles, the prophets, the evangelists, the pastors and teachers, *and the missionaries*," and since the word *missionary* does not occur in the Bible, it should be obvious that *missionary call* will not appear either. However, building upon this observation, some have concluded that there is no legitimate call to missions; it is simply a choice that is available to anyone. Proponents of this perspective say that just as you may choose to be a plumber or banker, you may choose to be a missionary.

The second perspective on the missionary call is that there is indeed such a call, and everyone already has it, referring to the Great Commission. This perspective is seen in the challenge from missionary martyr Jim Elliot, when he encouraged young people to go to the mission fields, saying, "We don't need a call; we need a kick in the pants."[1] However, it is hardly accurate to say that God has called all to go. Paul asked in Romans 10:15a, "And how are they to preach unless they are sent?" He is clearly teaching that some are to stay behind to send, pray, give, and enable those whom God calls to go.

A third perspective is that there is indeed a very specific, personal, and particular call; but the world is such a dangerous place, if you do not know for certain that you have been called, you had better not try to go. However, those advocating this perspective quickly add that if you do have such a call, you had better not try to stay; just ask Jonah when you get to heaven! God does indeed have a unique will for everyone, including the missionary call for many of His children. Additionally, the missionary call finds fulfillment in a multitude of diverse expressions according to His exact guidance— which is just as unique as the call.

This confusion about the missionary call has kept many off the missionary field. It also contributes to the confusion on the mission field regarding the task of missions. We often fail to appreciate the fact that God calls His people to do His will in His way in the places He chooses. God may call one to a ministry of rescuing orphans and child prostitutes in India as He did Amy Carmichael, another to translate the Bible into previously unwritten languages as he did Cam Townsend, and yet another to evangelize and teach indigenous peoples in America as He did David Brainerd. Each of them faithfully fulfilled God's missionary call in their lives as He guided them.

What has God called missionaries to do? There is not simply one expression of the missionary call for every missionary. Failure to discern God's specific, peculiar, personal call and failure to allow others to be divinely guided to express their calling differently often results in harsh judgment of other missionaries. When this happens, we may see some as not being faithful to the missionary task—not realizing that we have defined it too narrowly.

WHAT ABOUT PAUL?

When debating the biblical role of missionaries—such as whether to reach and leave or to reach and teach—someone will inevitably ask, "What about Paul?" Interestingly, proponents from both sides of the argument appeal to Paul as the biblical model for the position they have taken. There is wisdom and safety in appealing to the Scriptures for guidance in faith and practice. However, many claim Paul as their model without understanding what the Bible teaches about him and his ministry. Let's go back to the Bible and ask, "So, what about Paul?"

Paul provides a brief overview of his life in Philippians 3:5–6, "Circumcised on the eighth day, of the people of Israel, of the tribe of Benjamin, a Hebrew of Hebrews; as to the law, a Pharisee; as to zeal, a persecutor of the church; as to righteousness, under the law blameless." Paul was zealous for the law and the purity of Judaism, so much so that he writes in Galatians 1:14, "And I was advancing in Judaism beyond many of my own age among my people, so extremely zealous was I for the traditions of my fathers." Paul was a Pharisee who was converted while on a trip to Damascus where he was hoping to find more Christians to persecute. Jesus stopped Paul in his pursuit and persecution of believers, saved him, and gave him his own missionary call (Acts 9:1–19; 22:21).

PAUL'S MISSIONARY MINISTRY

Paul began to preach the gospel that he had previously sought to silence. As he did so, he became the human instrument that God used in the advance of the kingdom more than any other sinner saved by grace. It is understandable that the churches were hesitant to receive him, based on his activities prior to his conversion. However, he eventually became a powerful teacher of the Word. Indeed, when Barnabas went to Antioch to investigate the rumors of multicultural church growth, he realized that they needed more teachers and preachers and went to Tarsus to find Paul so he could join him in the teaching ministry of that church (Acts 11:19–26).

The church at Antioch was the first multicultural and intentionally international missionary church. It was there that believers first began to share the gospel with Greek-speaking Gentiles. The believers in Antioch were so serious about their faith and being conformed to the image of Christ that the pagans coined the derisive term *Christian* to describe them. Antioch is also the church that received the instruction from the Holy Spirit to send Paul and Barnabas on the first missionary journey. It is not insignificant that the first multicultural body of Christ was also the first missionary-sending church and that it was this same body that had sat under the teaching of Paul and Barnabas for an entire year.

The first missionary journey occurred in AD 46–47 and is described in Acts 13–14. The Bible reveals the route they traveled and notes some of their experiences, but it describes very little regarding their philosophy, strategy, or methodology of missions. They evangelized, discipled, healed, ministered, and suffered persecution as they preached the gospel all the way to Derbe in Galatia. Then they retraced their steps in a reverse route and encouraged all the believers to remain faithful and be ready for persecution. It is noteworthy that even on such a short journey, they appointed elders in every church and with prayer and fasting committed them to the Lord (Acts 14:23). However, Paul's continuing concern for the churches is obvious. Even though they had visited the churches once, Paul and Barnabas took the time to return to Lystra, Iconium, and Antioch. Their sense of responsibility extended far beyond reaching and leaving. Although Paul and Barnabas began their ministry in the synagogues, they were also intentionally reaching out to Gentiles. This bold evangelism among Gentiles drew the attention and ire of many in Judaism. The uproar resulted in a council that was held in Jerusalem (Acts 15:1–29).

Paul and Barnabas were present in the Jerusalem Council to defend the position that the gospel is for all peoples, not just the Jews, and that Gentiles should not have to become Jews to come to Christ. The council supported this position and sent an open letter to announce their decision. Not only did the church leaders agree with the missionaries that Gentiles could come to Christ without having to become good Jews first, they sent Paul and Barnabas as their spokesmen to deliver this verdict to the churches. The elders also commended Paul and Barnabas for risking their lives for the gospel and affirmed their ministry among the Gentiles. Paul and Barnabas then returned to Antioch to preach and teach the believers there.

The second missionary journey took place in AD 49–51 and is described in Acts 15:35–18:17. On this trip, Paul traveled in order to encourage the believers and churches from the first missionary journey, but he had a new mission team. Paul and Barnabas parted company after a sharp disagreement regarding the continued use of John Mark, who had deserted them very early on the first trip. Barnabas, whose name means "son of encouragement" (Acts 4:36), proved true to his name again by seeking to restore John Mark. So Paul took Silas on this trip, picking up Timothy and Luke along the way to round out the mission team. It was on this trip that Paul learned to discern God's direction in ministry. This second missionary journey also included time in prison, an earthquake, conversions, witnessing at the Areopagus, and as always, teaching.

Paul's third missionary journey took place in AD 52–57 and is described in Acts 18:23–21:16. The fact that he pastored and taught new believers in Ephesus for at least two years explains why this was the longest of Paul's missionary journeys. Interestingly, even though Paul spent significant time in Ephesus teaching and discipling, he did not consider the work there complete. In fact, even after Paul left Ephesus, he sent Timothy back for the express purpose of overseeing what was being taught (1 Timothy 1:3). The third missionary journey was filled with extraordinary missionary experiences: demon possession, radical conversion of sorcerers, a riot, an assassination plot against the missionary, raising a young man from the dead, and again, teaching.

Paul's Writing Ministry

In addition to the information that Luke provides about Paul and his ministry in the book of Acts, the Bible contains thirteen letters that Paul wrote to the churches to teach them what they were to believe and do. He wrote the letters to encourage, to correct, and to rebuke at times, but always to teach right doctrine and practice for disciples of Christ. Benjamin Merkle explains Paul's use of letters in his ministry to the Ephesians, the church with whom he spent the most time: "Approximately fifteen years after planting a church in Ephesus, Paul, through his co-worker Timothy, wrote to encourage and strengthen the church. They still needed help in appointing leaders (overseers/elders and deacons), stopping the false teachers, and protecting the gospel."[2] This was not the only church to receive such attention and concern from Paul.

IN EPHESIANS 4, Paul says that God has given leaders, evangelists, and teachers so that there will be unity and maturity in the church and "so that we may no longer be children, tossed to and fro by the waves and carried about by every wind of doctrine by human cunning, by craftiness in deceitful schemes" (verse 14). Theological education advances unity, maturity, and biblical discernment—all three of which are vital for combating errors. As in Paul's day, there is false teaching on every side in the field today, and unless we promote theological education we will leave believers unprotected from "every wind" of error.

—BRIAN VICKERS

Associate Professor of New Testament Interpretation, The Southern Baptist Theological Seminary

The open sins of the Corinthian church members made their way to the ears of Paul and broke his heart. He responded with a letter that denounced the sins and gave clear instruction as to how the church should handle those who had sinned. Sexual sins in the Corinthian church were a constant struggle, perhaps as a result of their cultural background. This is illustrative of the reality that cultures and worldviews influence the forms of Christianity around the world and that missionaries must maintain constant vigilance to avoid syncretism and heresy. Paul always made sure he had a voice in the purity of the belief and practice of the churches he planted. He would not simply plant a church and leave without this oversight.

Paul could not limit his career to a lifetime of service in one church, but neither did he abandon one in order to move on to another. Paul wrote letters to continue training and providing guidance for the churches. Merkle emphasizes the purpose of this ministry: "Paul's letter writing, then, demonstrates his concern for the on-going growth of the churches he planted. His goal was not merely to plant churches and let them loose, regardless of the consequences. Rather, Paul wisely maintained a healthy ongoing relationship with his churches so that the work of the gospel continued to flourish."[3] In addition to the use of correspondence, when Paul became aware of specific ongoing problems within churches needing intervention, he often not only sent a letter but also a ministry partner to serve on the field alongside the church. Through letters or disciples that he sent to teach and pastor, Paul watched over the churches and exercised loving parental care over them. Clearly, Paul desired sound doctrine in the churches, and he continued to train and edify them even from a distance.

WAS PAUL A MISSIONARY?

Someone has said that a missionary is "anyone who cannot get used to the sound of pagan footsteps on their way to a Christless eternity." When using a broad definition like this, we would have to say that of course Paul was a missionary. In fact, using a broad understanding of the term, the great English Baptist preacher of the nineteenth century Charles Haddon Spurgeon once said, "Every Christian is either a missionary or an imposter."[4] His point was that all true believers should have hearts that long for the salvation of lost people everywhere. However, we need to define the term more precisely, or everyone and no one is a missionary.

Defining Missionary

A technical definition begins with the etymology of the word. The word *missionary* comes from a Latin word meaning "to send"; therefore, a missionary is "a sent one." However, a fair question— and the one which this book addresses—is, "*Sent* to do what?" Paul writes in 2 Corinthians 5 that Christians are ambassadors for Christ, sent with the ministry and message of reconciliation: preaching the gospel, making disciples, and teaching disciples to observe all that Christ has commanded us. Certainly, this should be true in the life of a missionary, a *sent one.*

A proper definition of the term *missionary* distinguishes the missionary from an evangelist or preacher by including the idea of crossing boundaries for the sake of the gospel. These boundaries may be linguistic, geopolitical, socioeconomic, or cultural. In our modern age of globalization, one does not have to cross salt water to be a missionary. There are people groups traveling and living all over the world, bringing their languages, worldviews, religions, and cultures with them. Regardless of where you live in today's world, you will find people nearby who identify with other languages and cultures. God provides intercultural ministry opportunities in virtually every corner of the world.

If a missionary is someone who intentionally crosses boundaries to share the gospel, make and teach disciples, and plant churches among them, then Paul was clearly a missionary. John Polhill writes, "No description fits Paul better than that of missionary. Acts consistently portrays him in this role. The patterns of missionary activity established by Paul are in many aspects still followed today."[5] The Lord Jesus sent Paul to take the gospel to the Gentiles (Acts 13:47;

22:21; 26:17), and the Bible is clear that Paul faithfully discharged his duty and sought to fulfill this calling. Paul was so evidently a missionary that Barnett writes, "Paul the missionary became the great example for centuries of those who would leave the security and comfort of home for the perils and uncertainty of the itinerant missionary."[6]

WAS PAUL AN INTERCULTURAL MISSIONARY?

In order to answer the question of whether Paul was an inter-cultural missionary, it is necessary to define a couple of additional terms. First, the field of missiology is relatively new when compared with the rest of the theological encyclopedia. As such, the discipline's taxonomy has been growing, subdividing, and developing as missiologists have needed more precise and technical descriptors in order to communicate. The term *cross-cultural* has historically referred to anything or anyone that crosses from one culture to another. However, this was not precise enough for clear communication. Missiologists needed a way to refer to what is true in multiple cultures as well as the dynamics related to crossing from one culture to another —as missionaries do. In the most recent literature, cross-cultural refers to that which is true or exists in multiple cultures. Intercultural refers to crossing from one culture into another or many others. For instance, since a child's love for his mother and a mother's care for her baby are universal, these are cross-cultural realities; they cross all cultures. However, the work of Canadian UN doctors and nurses treating patients in Uganda is intercultural medical work. For this same reason, intercultural is the term used to describe the ministry of missionaries who have crossed cultural boundaries for the sake of the gospel.

What then are these cultural boundaries? Culture is the sum total of the rules of the game of life as it is played by the ethnic groups around the world. Cultures are not innate; they are learned from parents, siblings, friends, and society. These shared understandings are then passed on to others, from one generation to another. For instance, an adopted Chinese baby raised in a typical North American family in the USA would not grow up speaking Mandarin or Cantonese, using chopsticks, and preferring Confucianism. She would learn the worldview, language, greetings, and culturally appropriate rules for acting, reacting, and interacting from her new family and environment.

One of the most basic levels of culture is language. Indeed, cultural anthropologists often refer to people groups as ethnolinguistic groups. God is the author of this language development in the history of the cultures of man. After man rebelled and failed to fulfill God's command to fill the earth, He dispersed the people according to languages at the Tower of Babel. This is the beginning of the myriad cultures and their differences found in the world today. While there are many diverse markers that distinguish cultures, language is certainly one of the most basic. The theories of linguistic relativism and linguistic determinism focus on the extent to which languages shape or influence the people who speak them. Using the linguistic challenges alone, one can see the cultural barrier in Acts 14:8–18. There, God used Paul and Barnabas to heal a man who had been lame from birth. The people mistakenly attributed the healing power to their own gods, and shouting in their own language, they called the men Zeus and Hermes. Paul tried his best to communicate to them that they were just men. However, "even with these words they scarcely restrained the people from offering sacrifice to them" (Acts 14:18).

Let us then define an intercultural missionary in this way: *one whom God has called and sent as an ambassador of Christ with the message of reconciliation to make disciples, baptize, and teach to obey all that He has commanded, and who intentionally crosses cultural boundaries to do so.* The life of David Brainerd illustrates the fact that one does not have to cross salt water to fulfill such a calling. He engaged Native American indigenous peoples, learned their language and culture, and preached the gospel in such extreme conditions as to hasten a premature death. Countless other missionaries in the pages of history crossed cultural barriers, learned languages, suffered persecution, planted churches, discipled, and taught indigenous pastors who converted from paganism—all without ever leaving the shores of their home continent.

The apostle Paul was a missionary who crossed boundaries of many kinds: cultural, linguistic, worldview, religious adherence, geographical, and socioeconomic. Eckhard Schnabel writes, "Paul was bicultural both in the cognitive and in the functional sense. As a Jew whose family maintained conservative 'Hebrew' traditions while living in the Greek Diaspora city of Tarsus, Paul understood both Jewish and Greco-Roman cultures. He was at least bilingual, probably trilingual: he was fluent in Aramaic and in Greek, and in all probability also in Hebrew. He was evidently able to function comfortably, without consciously 'crossing over' into one or the other culture, both in Jewish culture and in Greco-Roman culture."[7] Paul was indeed multilingual and could very likely move easily across several cultures, yet he was forced to work across some cultural and worldview lines that perfectly describe intercultural missions (Acts 14:8–18; 17:22–34; 18:1–8; 21:37–40).

When one considers the culture, mores, worldview, and socioeconomic worlds of Martha's Vineyard, Cajun Louisiana, inner-city gangs in Los Angeles, and the proverbial Mayberrys of the United States, it is easy to see that many cultures and subcultures may share the same country and yet be very distinct. Indeed, they also may share the same language, currency, laws, calendar, and holidays, yet be worlds apart in virtually every aspect of life. A young missionary from any one of those backgrounds going to any of the others would find many barriers to cross in order to communicate the gospel effectively in culturally appropriate ways.

Some have questioned whether Paul was an intercultural missionary or simply an itinerant preacher and evangelist. Polhill writes, "Paul was in every sense a 'pioneer' missionary."[8] This international ministry included preaching the gospel to many subcultures, worldviews, and a diversity of religious adherents. The apostle Paul may have been a Roman citizen speaking several languages, thoroughly grounded in Judaism (though raised among Hellenists), but as he traveled and ministered throughout the Roman empire he would have encountered countless cultures from region to region, circumcised to uncircumcised, synagogue to pagan temple, and foods ranging from kosher to pork. Paul Barnett writes, "From the beginnings of his new missionary thrust, Paul adopted new approaches. He established churches in rapid succession as a means of spreading the gospel locally; he drew others into partnership with him as traveling coworkers and as envoys; he pioneered letter writing as a means of instructing his churches in absentia. By far the most significant difference, however, was his deliberate outreach to rank pagans, idol worshipping, temple-attending Gentiles. Soon his churches were mainly composed of such Gentiles as well, no doubt, as synagogue-connected Godfearers."[9]

The apostle Paul was, by all practical definitions, a man who crossed many different boundaries for the sake of the gospel. Schnabel summarizes the goals of Paul's missiological method:

> First, Paul knew himself to be called to preach the message of Jesus Christ. . . . Second, Paul knew himself particularly called to preach the gospel of Jesus Christ to the Gentiles, that is, to polytheists who worshiped other gods. . . . Third, Paul's goal was to reach as many people as possible. . . . Fourth, Paul seeks to lead individual people to believe in the one true God and in Jesus Christ, the Messiah, Savior and Lord. . . . Fifth, Paul established new churches among the followers of Jesus Christ—both Jews and Gentiles, men and women, free and slaves—and teaches the new believers the Word of God, the teachings of Jesus, the significance of the gospel for everyday living.[10]

Paul moved from region to region throughout the Roman Empire, preaching, discipling, and church planting. He was a tentmaker (literally) for a time to support his ministry. He struggled to understand and be understood—at least among those speaking the Lycaonian language—and was required to speak more than one language in his ministry—Greek, Aramaic, and very likely Hebrew as well. Paul very intentionally preached in synagogues and yearned to see his Jewish brothers come to Christ and be saved. He also argued for Gentiles to be accepted without converting to Judaism first, even helping Ephesians and Corinthians to contextualize the gospel and apply the teachings of the Bible. Paul was clearly an intercultural missionary.

OVERVIEW OF PAUL'S MISSIONARY METHODOLOGY

Rather than speculate, "What would Paul do?" to devise our strategies, we should focus our consideration on what Paul actually did. Paul emphasized that his ministry was to proclaim the whole counsel of the Word of God in synagogues, in the streets, and from house to house. Roland Allen says that Paul did not have a predetermined strategy that guided his decisions for travel: "We have seen that he did not start out with any definite design to establish his churches in this place or in that. He was led as God opened the door; but wherever he was led he always found a centre, and seizing upon that centre he made it a centre of Christian life."[11] Certainly, the Holy Spirit guided him in what he did and where he went, as we see in Acts 16:6–10.

Paul was concerned with much more than simply evangelizing and forming these believers into churches—he wanted them to know and live out the truth. Schnabel wrote of Paul's focus among the churches, "Paul describes himself as a teacher 'in every church' (1 Corinthians 4:17). His rulings on theological and ethical questions are relevant for 'all the churches' (1 Corinthians 7:17; cf. 11:16; 14:33; 16:1). Paul's letters reveal the following focal points: theological instruction, ethical instruction, instruction concerning the life of the church, and evangelistic outreach."[12] Surely, the overarching reason for Paul's concern was his zeal for the truth. Paul's constant exposure to pagan religions and cultures everywhere he traveled must have made him keenly aware of the great risk of syncretism in new churches. It was this awareness combined with his zeal for the truth that led to his consistent and early focus on doctrinal instruction for believers. Schnabel declares, "A first major focus was the theological instruction of believers."[13]

When Paul could not be personally present, he sent prepared teachers to complete the work in young churches. Paul consistently employed young disciples such as Tychicus, Timothy, and Titus in such ministries. Although Paul's practice was to appoint elders for the churches, there were times when he left or sent these disciples to continue the work of training and appointing elders (Acts 14:23; Titus 2:1, 15). In a sense, these young disciples were an extension and a continuation of Paul's ministry. He could travel to minister elsewhere knowing that these men could continue grounding new believers in truth.

PAUL'S MISSIONARY WORK "FULFILLED"

Continuing to answer the question, "What did Paul do?" leads to a consideration of Paul's understanding of fulfilling the work God gave him. In Romans 15:19, he wrote, "By the power of signs and wonders, by the power of the Spirit of God—so that from Jerusalem and all the way around to Illyricum I have fulfilled the ministry of the gospel of Christ." Paul spoke of fulfillment, even though he revealed throughout his writings that the formation of Christ in the lives of the believers through sound teaching and practice was a lifelong ministry concern. Commenting on Romans 15:19, Merkle wrote, "His statement must be understood to mean that as God's apostle to the Gentiles, he has fulfilled his apostolic obligation to start new evangelistic work in the regions from Jerusalem to Illyricum. The Greek word translated 'fulfilled' can also be translated 'completed.' By preaching the gospel and establishing churches in all the various regions, in one sense Paul had 'completed the gospel.' Yet as a well-balanced missionary, Paul did not simply move on and abandon his previous works."[14] Missionaries who seek to model their lives and ministries after the apostle Paul should seek to reach and teach instead of merely reaching and leaving—even if the teaching requires other teachers who follow the pioneer preacher.

Paul was also interested in the unreached people groups and regions, as he revealed in the very next verse, "Thus I make it my ambition to preach the gospel, not where Christ has already been named, lest I build on someone else's foundation" (Romans 15:20). With this desire, God used Paul to fulfill prophecy: "So shall he sprinkle many nations; kings shall shut their mouths because of him; for that which has not been told them they see, and that which they have not heard they understand" (Isaiah 52:15). However, Paul's missiological method included more than simply preaching. As has been clearly seen, this was only the beginning aspect of his ministry in these places.

Polhill comments on Paul's desire to move on to new areas although burdened for sound theology and churches among new believers. "Paul was often torn between his urgent call to establish new work and his concern for the well-being of the congregations he had already founded."[15] Certainly, Paul wanted to preach the gospel as often as he could to as many as possible; but he knew that a faithful minister should ground people in the truth as well. Instead of reaching, preaching, and leaving, Paul revisited the churches in Galatia and Achaia and even stayed to pastor the churches in Corinth and Ephesus for many months. He pored over the reports that came to him from the churches he had started, and he wrote letters to rebuke, correct, and exhort. Indeed, Schnabel stated, "Paul's main concern evidently was not to reach as many people as quickly as possible with the gospel."[16] Paul stated that he longed to preach Christ in the unreached areas so that he would not be building on another man's foundation, but his ministry reveals that this was balanced with staying to preach and teach, writing letters, or sending disciples in his place to continue the essential ministry that remained.

PAUL'S MISSIONARY STRATEGY AND MINISTRY

Paul's missiological method was intercultural and international, and it sought to evangelize, preach, and teach the Word of God. J. Knox Chamblin notes, "According to Paul, being made whole entails an encounter with the triune God; and this occurs, by God's own design, through God's revealed Word."[17] Paul did not preach a thin gospel, one sermon built on a single passage, delivered in the same fashion to the cookie-cutter audiences. Paul's teaching ministry incorporated the whole counsel of the word of God taught to people of every culture he encountered—Jew and Greek, barbarian and Scythian, and slave and free. Schnabel summarizes Paul's missiological method: "The basic strategy of Paul was simple: he wanted to proclaim the message of Jesus Christ to Jews and Gentiles in obedience to a divine commission, particularly in areas in which it had not been proclaimed before (Galatians 2:7; Romans 15:14–21). The planning for the implementation of this goal likewise was relatively simple: he traveled on the major Roman roads and on smaller local roads from city to city, preaching the message of Jesus the Messiah and Savior and gathering new converts into local Christian communities."[18] While Paul's strategy was simple, it was not simplistic. He became all things to all men and used all means to reach and teach them for the sake of the gospel.

Paul understood that responsible missions work would not allow his desire to move quickly to new areas to jettison his duty to train trainers, educate educators, and disciple disciplers. Paul wrote in 2 Timothy 2:2, "And what you have heard from me in the presence of many witnesses entrust to faithful men who will be able to teach others also." Paul understood that he would not live on earth forever and that the churches needed sound teachers of the truth. Therefore, he knew that it was not enough to train the pastors; he also needed to train trainers and instill in them an awareness of the need to train still more.

Paul knew that he needed to train the young disciples whom the Holy Spirit was calling so that they could continue the work. In addition to basic discipleship, Paul prepared teachers to be able to teach sound doctrine in the churches he started and those that would be planted by them. Theological education as part of the missionary task is neither a luxury nor optional; it is the duty of all responsible missionaries. While the pioneer missionary may not stay to bring this to completion, he should prepare "Timothys," or facilitate the arrival of other missionaries to prepare them, before he leaves.

There must be pastoral preparation and theological education of the disciples who take over. Merkle wrote,

> The goal of theological education in missions is to strengthen the local believers to do the work of the ministry. It is not about controlling the local believers or even indoctrinating them. It is, rather, empowering them with the Word of God, which liberates them in their service to God and to others. It is about passing on what we have learned to other faithful men who will do the same. It is about training local Bible teachers who can help train the next generations of pastors. It is about training missionaries who will go out into the harvest fields. It is about training scholars who will be able to translate the Bible into their own language or write theological literature that will be used to educate others. It is about preventing the tempter from stealing the fruit of our labor lest we labor in vain.[19]

Paul modeled and instructed the church to equip faithful trainers who would be able to continue the work of training future generations of believers. Not only can they train future leaders, trained national teachers incorporate their understanding of the language, culture, worldview, and history that an outside missionary will never completely know.

CONCLUSION

Paul is the greatest missionary who ever lived. He set the standard, and he is our biblical model for crossing cultural boundaries to reach, preach, and teach. Both those who stress going to preach where Christ has not been named and those who stress the need to use every means to train nationals in sound doctrine and the ability to teach others may rightly claim Paul as their model.

Was Paul only interested in preaching in areas where no one had ever heard of Jesus or the gospel? No, of course not; Paul also emphasized sound teaching, ethical instruction, and culturally appropriate application for sound theology among the churches. In addition, he stressed the importance of having biblically qualified and theologically prepared leadership in the churches. Merkle summarizes the argument well: "Let us learn from the Church's greatest missionary and have a balanced approach to missions—one that both pushes back the darkness by engaging unreached people groups with the gospel and also keeps the darkness back by leaving behind a church that is mature and able effectively to grow and reproduce."[20]

The New Testament record of Paul's life demonstrates his balanced desire to reach the unreached, as well as to train the reached so that he could leave behind him doctrinally sound churches with biblically qualified and trained leadership. Modeling Paul's practice of training young men and sending them into ministry situations multiplies our ministries and allows us to continue reaching into new areas without abandoning untaught new believers. It also utilizes trained local leadership and empowers them to preach, teach, pastor, and disciple among themselves in culturally appropriate ways.

Suggested Reading

Allen, Roland. *Missionary Methods: St. Paul's or Ours?* Cambridge: Lutterworth Press, 2006.

Barnett, Paul. *Paul: Missionary of Jesus.* Vols. 1–2. Grand Rapids: Eerdmans, 2008.

Chamblin, J. Knox. *Paul and the Self: Apostolic Teaching for Personal Wholeness.* Grand Rapids: Baker, 1993.

Dowsett, Rose. *The Great Commission.* Thinking Clearly Series. Grand Rapids: Kregel, 2001.

Merkle, Benjamin L. "The Need for Theological Education in Missions: Lessons Learned from the Church's Greatest Missionary." *The Southern Baptist Journal of Theology* 94:4 (Winter 2005): 50–61.

O'Brien, Peter. *Gospel and Mission in the Writings of Paul: An Exegetical and Theological Analysis.* Grand Rapids: Baker Books, 1995.

Polhill, John. *Paul and His Letters.* Nashville: B&H Publishers, 1999.

Schnabel, Eckhard J. *Early Christian Mission.* Vols. 1–2. Downers Grove, IL: InterVarsity Press, 2004.

_____. *Paul the Missionary: Realities, Strategies and Methods.* Downers Grove, IL: InterVarsity Press, 2008.

6

SEARCH VERSUS HARVEST THEOLOGY: REACHING OR TEACHING?

"No one deserves to hear the gospel twice until everyone has heard it once." This was the watchword in many missions rallies at the turn of the twentieth century. The slogan "The Evangelization of the World in This Generation" was the rallying cry of J. R. Mott, chairman of the Student Volunteer movement in the late 1800s, who also emphasized this perspective. While the command to share the gospel with every person on the planet has been in the Bible since the Gospels were written, the church has seldom agreed on a consistent balance and zeal to fulfill it.

Some missionaries and missions agencies seek not only to sow the seed but also to bring in the *harvest* of those who are coming to Christ in responsive areas. They preach the gospel, disciple believers, and plant churches. They develop primary schools, medical clinics, orphanages, and theological seminaries, and they form churches into associations and presbyteries. Other missionaries and mission agencies emphasize a *search* theology, which seeks to find and evangelize the pockets of peoples where no one has ever preached Christ. They build relationships, evangelize, and reach the unreached, only to leave as quickly as possible to reach others who have never heard the gospel. The continuum of biblical responsibilities and duties in the task of international missions includes both of these emphases; each is solidly biblical, and there is great danger when missionaries embrace one extreme and exclude the other.

The Bible clearly illustrates both areas of missions ministry, and missionaries should incorporate both to be balanced in their missiology, philosophies, strategies, and methodologies. The temptation to embrace either one of these extremes, to the exclusion of the other, often grows out of the failure to interpret the Word of God correctly. For instance, an eschatologically driven missiology that springs from faulty hermeneutics could result in missionaries zealously seeking to honor God in ways He never intended. Giving biblical authority to our own definitions of extrabiblical terms also results in confusion and division between those who embrace our opinion and those who do not.

Additionally, choosing a few specific passages to define our ministry, instead of the whole counsel of the Word of God, may result in ministry imbalance, for us and for those who follow us. Was Paul more concerned with Romans 15:20, "And thus I make it my ambition to preach the gospel, not where Christ has already been named, lest I build on someone else's foundation," or 2 Timothy 2:2, "And what you have heard from me in the presence of many witnesses entrust to faithful men who will be able to teach others also"? Since the Holy Spirit inspired Paul to write both, there must be a balance. Understanding this biblical balance will prevent us from streamlining our mission efforts to emphasize one extreme at the exclusion of the other.

DEVELOPMENT OF THE DEFINITIONS

As mission agencies began to reach into the unreached pockets to fulfill the task of the Great Commission, limitations of human and financial resources frustrated their efforts. Trying to determine which areas of the world were "reached" enough for missionaries to move on was frustrating. For instance, in some areas, there might have been only one small church, but it possessed trained leadership and vibrant evangelism, and it seemed to be advancing. However, none of those criteria were objective or easily quantifiable. Missiologists came to believe that they needed to adopt a commonly accepted percentage criterion for considering a people group reached. With such a criterion in place, missionaries would have a goal to work toward and a clear conscience if they left once they attained the percentage.

A FORMULAIC APPROACH to missions that places a high premium on rapidly abandoning tried and tested practices in favor of cutting-edge discoveries in the social sciences or the business world has not benefited missions in the majority world. Instead, the pursuit of efficiency in missions has left behind a trail of broken relationships. Established missions decisively cease further assistance to their spiritual children, the fruit of their earlier missions, in the name of prioritizing time and resources for unreached people groups. The spiritual children are denied the opportunity to transform from dependent to equal partner in missions as the parent "adopts" new children. The "either/or" language used by many Western missions is polarizing and unhelpful. We create false dichotomies between older mission paradigms and newer ones. We need to use a "both/and" language more. Both traditional methods and new thinking and strategies are essential to the fulfilling of the Great Commission today.

—Fong Choon Sam
Professor of Missions,
Baptist Theological Seminary, Singapore

Initially, missionaries were working with the figure of 20 percent evangelical as sufficient to consider a group reached; this was based on a sociological axiom that if 20 percent of a population accepts a new idea, the adopters can perpetuate and propagate it within the group without outside help. Missionaries made the application that if a group was at least 20 percent evangelical, this group could continue the work of evangelism without the help of outside missionaries, thus freeing the missionaries to move on.

Yet, what really precipitated the need for the percentage? More important, how did the percentage that missions researchers deem necessary for self-propagation drop so drastically? In most missions circles, it has become a "fact" as widely accepted as the laws of physics that when a people group's population is 2 percent evangelical, the missionaries can pass over them because they are considered reached. Many missiologists believe that the statistics reveal that the nationals can finish the missionary task without outside help. In the following pages, the architects and influencers in this strategic development describe its development in their own words.

Interestingly, not even those who devised and promoted the idea of identifying the percentage of believers meant it to become a standard for deciding where missionaries should serve; it was merely to be a benchmark for discerning the least reached. Patrick Johnstone, best known as author of *Operation World*, stated,

From what I remember it all started with someone using a secular market research figure that there needed to be 20% of a population affected to actually change their society. This then came to be thought of as the target to be Christian to qualify as "reached." This then led to much discussion on what unreached might be. 20% was obviously not valid! One only has to think of Korea and Singapore and vibrant missions-sending countries with around that level of Christian population. A number of people pushed for 5% or maybe a 2% Christian as the minimum for qualification for "reached." I personally do not like the term "reached," but have to live with it. It was a battle I fought, but did not, in this case, win![1]

Continuing to reflect on the progression of the strategy, Johnstone admitted, "It had been decided several years before that for the remaining years of this millennium we needed to make a strategic limitation of the peoples to those over 10,000 population and under 5% Christian or 2% evangelical, and also to limit our listing to peoples defined by ethnicity or language. The cut-off points were reasonable, but arbitrary."[2]

The strategic cut-off points were not the only aspects of the discussions that were arbitrary and subjective. Johnstone continued,

> Then came the big question, "What IS a Christian?" To many mission bodies this meant, by implication, evangelicals. The problem was that only two people in the world had ever done any real research that could stand up to scientific scrutiny to count evangelicals—myself and David Barrett. . . . So I then pressed in both Lausanne and then AD2000 discussions that we must NOT rely on evangelical figures, but use the wider "Christian" appellation which includes all six major streams of Christianity (including Catholics and Mormons!), for these figures are more readily available and are based on the real or potential self-declaration of individuals (in censuses or polls), and, further, you cannot treat a pious Catholic country as non-Christian! It was I who suggested a compromise of any people below either 5% Christian OR 2% evangelical should be considered unreached to the extent that there were likely not to be the resources within that population segment to completely evangelize every part of that segment without outside (missionary) help.[3]

The Joshua Project concurs with Johnstone's argument. "The original Joshua Project editorial committee selected the criteria less than 2% evangelical Christian and less than 5% Christian adherents. While these percentage figures are somewhat arbitrary, there are some that suggest that the percentage of a population needed to be influenced to impact the whole group is 2%."[4]

In a recent interview, Greg Parsons, general director of Ralph

Winter's US Center for World Mission, provided additional details surrounding the historical framework for evaluating levels of missions focus and need on the basis of whether a people group is at least 2 percent evangelical. This statistical criterion was associated with quantifying the fulfillment of producing a viable indigenous evangelizing church movement. Producing such a movement was the goal of the AD2000 Movement, and it was the leadership of the Movement who recognized the need to create a means by which achievement of the goal could be applied on the ground of any given people group. They not only had to consider whether to quantify the progress but also how to do so.

Luis Bush, using information from Patrick Johnstone's *Operation World* data, began to evaluate language and classifications. The original starting point was World Vision's classification of those groups with less than 20 percent Christian population as "hidden peoples." When Bush and the AD2000 Movement were reconsidering or refining the measurements for their purposes, it is believed that they looked back to this statistic as the beginning point for the discussions on quantifying vulnerability. Additionally, Patrick Johnstone reported that the group discussed the realities of what was happening in various parts of the world and realized that there were indigenous church planting movements going on in places where far fewer than 20 percent of the population was Christian. Through discussions with Luis Bush and Patrick Johnstone, the AD2000 Movement leadership eventually agreed on the statistical criteria of 2 percent evangelical or 5 percent Christian as the minimum numbers necessary to produce a viable indigenous evangelizing church movement. It was this same group who also agreed on the uniform use of the term "unreached people group" instead of the previously used "hidden peoples." It is significant that the context of the discussions was never to classify whether an individual was reached or not, but rather which groups were unreached. The definitions and statistical criteria were a collective assessment of how to define a group of people for the purpose of resources and focus. Parsons indicated that in the

1990s, the AD2000 Movement was simply looking for something that was more easily able to be measured.[5]

The combination of measuring the strength and viability of Christian populations, the emergence of people group thinking, and the need for speed driven by eschatological missiology has created the perfect storm. The result is a missions philosophy that determines strategy, deploys missionaries, and invests missions resources based on arbitrarily determined levels of "reachedness." Interestingly, in an article that describes the development of unreached people group thinking and includes a list of UPGs at various levels of reachedness, Dan Scribner wrote,

> What the list is NOT—This list is NOT a comprehensive unreached peoples listing. This is not meant to be the "end-all" list. Rather, it is the result of merging major streams of unreached peoples research and determining certain parameters such as the ethno-linguistic-political criteria and other considerations such as greater than 10,000 population and most needy of the gospel. It should also NOT be assumed that the Great Commission would be fulfilled if every one of these groups had a viable, reproducing church capable of reaching the rest of this people. No one is predicting closure once the last group on this list is engaged and penetrated.[6]

However, some mission agencies who are striving to usher in the kingdom of God more rapidly have utilized the list precisely in this way.

REACHED AND UNREACHED

While missionaries once argued about the relative value of search versus harvest theologies, they now debate in terms of reached versus unreached to address many of the same points. Of course, to consider working among the reached or unreached, we have to define the terms.

Who is a Christian? Some missiologists consider only baptized members of evangelical churches to be Christians, while others use the word for anyone who self-identifies as Christian. This would include many who are ethnically Christian—those who were born in a "Christian" village as opposed to a "Muslim" village. They also include members of any cult or aberrant form of Christianity without consideration of biblical definitions. The problem is that the number of evangelical Christians in a population is difficult to ascertain. Statistics for self-identifying Christians are easier to obtain and are preferred by some researchers—especially those who are comfortable with ecumenical understandings of Christianity. Todd Johnson, director of the Center for the Study of Global Christianity and co-author of *World Christian Encyclopedia*, stated, "Every people group in the world is unreached from someone's point of view. The 5 percent criteria changes that dynamic because it says there is no such thing as a 'Christian' unreached people."[7] While this makes it easier for a researcher to report the number of Christians in an area, such data would be useless or misleading to those who define true Christians only in evangelical terms. Many missionaries would not accept Johnson's conclusion, "If a people group is 1 percent evangelical and 95 percent Roman Catholic it is not an unreached people group. It may need church planting, but does not need frontier missions."[8]

Even allowing arbitrary percentages of "Christianity" to determine whether a group is unreached or not, the confusion remains. Not being "unreached" does not equal being "reached." Even the influential voices in the conversations about levels of reachedness are not recommending disengagement once Christians reach an arbitrary percentage of the population. The issue is more accurately one of emphasis and resources. Todd Johnson stated, "Oftentimes when peoples are already reached and where there are many resources, there is a strong emphasis on saturation church planting. At the same time, in frontier missions, even by mission agencies such as the IMB, there are few resources and few churches. Consequently there is little sense in shutting down a tiny operation when it crosses the 2 percent evangelical line."[9]

The assumption in efforts to classify levels of reachedness is that the less reached an area is, the more worthy it is of missionary investment. The pervasive thinking that the least reached should be our top priority leaves little room for the possibility that God might be leading someone to a harvest field. Even when God does so lead, missionaries sometimes feel inferior or guilty about not going to a search field. The Joshua Project promotes this mentality that has grown up in the modern era of people group thinking. Their well-intentioned zeal to reach the unreached has evolved into a missions value statement that considers the search fields to be the most worthy of missionary endeavor. Luis Bush wrote,

> Joshua Project 2000 is focused on the least-evangelized peoples of the world. At the heart of Joshua Project 2000 is a list of, what is currently, approximately 1,700 peoples that mission researchers have agreed upon as most needing a church-planting effort. Of these 1,700 peoples, numbering 2.2 billion people, nearly 90 percent of the individuals live in the 10/40 Window. . . . If we are to follow the example of Jesus who came "to seek and to save what was lost" (Luke 19:10) and who proclaimed that message to the poor (Luke 4:18), our primary concern will be the 10/40 Window where 99 percent of the world's least-evangelized poor can be found.[10]

Reaching the unreached with little thought to the value of staying to disciple and teach is an approach driven by the need for speed. The highest value for many is reaching as many as possible as fast as possible. This mentality is the missional groupthink that is the recurrent theme in missiology today, and it influences many missionary candidates as they seek to invest their lives in the places of greatest need. Cronk wrote, "With the publishing of the Joshua Project 2000 list, the nearly 2000 targeted least-evangelized peoples become clear pathways of service for a 'new missionary force.' Since denominations, local churches and mission agencies can now clearly and confidently use this list for adoption and prayer for the neediest least-evangelized peoples, the next step is to provide direct pathways of missions service among these peoples."[11]

The perspective that unreached areas are the places most worthy of investing your life in missions service grows out of the search theology, as if the harvest areas, where the churches need pastors and the pastors need training, are less important. Terms that describe the areas of greatest need sound romantic and adventurous, such as the *Last Frontier* and the *10/40 Window*. The Last Frontier refers to the areas of the world that are less than 2 percent evangelical and where virtually no church planting is taking place. They are considered unreached and unengaged people groups (UUPGs), and therefore the areas of greatest need. The 10/40 Window refers to an imaginary window on the globe stretching between ten and forty degrees north of the equator, and from West Africa to East Asia. This area is home to the world's greatest poverty, the majority of the adherents of world religions, and the fewest Christian resources and churches. The needs there are real, but emphasizing them while neglecting all else we have been called to do does not strengthen the church or render us faithful to the task He has given us.

Quite obviously, many missionaries allow search theology to drive their definition of the missionary task. Yet how can they consider the task of outside missionaries complete once two out of every one hundred people have prayed to receive Christ? Does such a low percentage of believers truly free the missionary to leave them for the next people group? What about the missionary task in the gospel-hostile places? One missionary working in North Africa reported that in the area of his ministry the life expectancy of a new believer is forty-five days. Are we really saying that two out of one hundred or even five out of one hundred can finish the task there?

Again, those who established the criteria for discerning the least reached people groups were not seeking to define the reached, much less were they determining whom we may abandon. But their research combined with need for speed drives many missionaries to find a way to abandon traditional missions models and complete the task. James Engel wrote, "I still hear many evangelicals calling to evangelize the maximum number of unreached people in the shortest possible time."[12] However, the biblical model would require us to slow down many current models rather than speed them up. Engel continued, "Missions would be better served by returning to the example of Jesus, who walked and lived among those whom he served, who took time to understand their spiritual awareness, fears, and dreams."[13]

Donald McGavran believed that effective missions strategy should respond to the receptivity of a people. "An essential task is to discern receptivity and—when this is seen—to adjust methods, institutions, and personnel until the receptive are becoming Christians and reaching out to win their fellows to eternal life. Effective evangelism is demanded. It finds the lost, folds those found, feeds them on the word of God, and incorporates them into multitudes of new and old congregations. That is why it is called effective evangelism."[14] In *Experiencing God*, Henry Blackaby championed the idea to find where God is working and join Him there. Alan Walker also wrote, "The task of the Christian is to find what God is doing, and do it with Him."[15] McGavran wrote that receptivity is not based on regions or countries but on the work of the Holy Spirit. "The receptivity or responsiveness of individuals waxes and wanes. No person is equally ready at all times to follow the way."[16]

HARVEST AND SEARCH THEOLOGIES

The terms *harvest theology* and *search theology*, introduced by Donald McGavran in *Understanding Church Growth*, are often opposite sides of the argument regarding where to invest missions' human and financial resources. Search theology stresses preaching Christ where He has not been named while harvest theology emphasizes bringing in the harvest among responsive people. When mission strategies embrace one approach to the exclusion of the other, an imbalance in missions is the result. Unfortunately, many missionaries have reached people groups and then hurriedly gone in search of UPGs, leaving unfinished work in the hands of untaught, ill-prepared national believers. The biblical approach is not either/or but both/ and, doing God's will where He leads according to His gifting. Paul wrote in Romans 12:6–7, "Having gifts that differ according to the grace given to us, let us use them: if prophecy, in proportion to our faith; if service, in our serving; the one who teaches, in his teaching." Each must be a faithful steward of the gifts God has entrusted to him. When God equips someone to teach, calls him to a teaching ministry, grants him a missionary call, and guides him to international service, no one should make that missionary feel inferior or ashamed for being faithful to God's gifting, calling, and guidance.

Harvest Arguments

The many aspects of working in the gospel-responsive areas of the world are primary concerns of harvest theology. McGavran wrote, "In many regions, missionaries must start the process; but it is clear that the gospel cannot be proclaimed to every creature, belief cannot become a real option to every person, until churches exist in all groupings of humanity, whether in city or country, or high or low caste, educated or illiterate, throughout the earth. Thus speaks a theology of harvest."[17] McGavran stressed the need for a harvest theology to complete the task Christ has given us: "One thing can delay a vast discipling of the peoples of the earth. If, in the day of harvest —the most receptive day God has yet granted for his church—his servants fail him, then the ripened grain will not be harvested."[18]

Building churches among every group enables the efficiency of the work of missions. As previously noted, McGavran recognized a homogeneous unit principle during his ministry among the peoples of India's castes. "People like to become Christians without crossing racial, linguistic, or class barriers."[19] That being true, missionaries should seek to plant culturally appropriate churches among the people groups of the world so that they can continue the work. Missionaries begin working in cities and countries with prayers and efforts to see the people come to Christ. Harvest theology proponents reason that the time to leave is not when God begins to answer their prayers and grant fruit to their efforts. In fact, as this phase begins, many see that their life work is just beginning. The desire of these missionaries to be good stewards and obedient servants leads them to recommit their lives and ministries in those very places.

SEARCH ARGUMENTS

Search theology is just as biblical as harvest theology in its desire to see God glorified in the world today. Proponents of this perspective look at the lands where the gospel has been preached and argue that these people have already heard the gospel. Moreover, many of them have turned a deaf ear to it. Missionaries also see that many of those who have heard and accepted Christ have been discipled, and therefore they ought to be able to tell the others. They believe that their own responsibility is to take the gospel message to those who have never heard.

Donald McGavran defined search theology in this way: "Christian outreach in today's responsive world demands a theology of harvest that the New Testament uniquely offers. Yet at this critical time, many Christians are firmly committed to a theology of seed sowing, which might also be called a theology of search. . . . It maintains that in evangelism the essential thing is not the finding, but going everywhere and preaching the gospel. . . ."[20] Widespread sowing of the seed is the essence of the missionary task for some. Others have argued that mere sowing is not wise when the soil in responsive areas awaits the seed. However, McGavran wrote, ". . . search theology fiercely attacked any emphasis on results."[21]

HOW HARVEST AND SEARCH THEOLOGIES WORK TOGETHER

It is a mistake to view harvest and search theologies as incompatible or mutually exclusive positions. God has called and equipped some missionaries to take the gospel to unreached unengaged areas of the world, while He has called others to disciple, teach, organize disciples into churches, and establish schools and support ministries. The areas of the world that have never heard must hear. Those that have heard must be discipled and taught all that Jesus has commanded. Those who have embraced Christianity need guides to help them continue the work until the day that the Holy Spirit leads the missionaries to other fields of service. Jerry Rankin, president of the International Mission Board, speaking of the need for the agency's reorganization in 1997, recognized the need to maintain a balance between harvest and search theologies in the missionary task. He wrote, "We have a tremendous force of dedicated, God-called missionaries who are serving effectively, but we believe we have been organized in a way that will not really stimulate the explosive growth we have the potential of seeing. We really need to become more focused than we have in the past on the harvest fields, on The Last Frontier, and on church growth."[22]

Eckhard Schnabel wrote that the apostle Paul did not minister from solely a harvest or a search theology; he sought the Spirit's guidance. "When it proved impossible for Paul to reach a region for which he had planned missionary outreach, as was the case with the project of traveling to the provinces of Asia, Bithynia, and Mysia (Acts 16:7–8), his strategy did not break down: there were other cities in other regions that needed to hear the gospel. Paul was prepared to leave the 'tactical selection' of locations for missionary work to God's sovereignty. He was willing to change plans. He depended not upon personal decisions but upon God's guidance."[23] Schnabel also noted, "Luke's account of Paul's missionary work confirms that the apostle did not limit his preaching to specific groups but targeted anyone who was willing to listen. . . . The geographical scope of Paul's missionary work was not controlled by a 'grand strategy' that helped him decide in which cities to begin a new missionary initiative. The evidence indicates that Paul moved to geographically adjacent areas that were open for missionary work."[24] It is a dangerous and unbiblical practice to emphasize one perspective to the exclusion of the other.

THE BIBLE AND THE BALANCE

Missiology that has been driven by eschatology has ranged from those who believe that Christ is returning any moment now—and so the church must reach as many as possible with the gospel so as to save as many as we can—to those who believe that He cannot return until the church on earth has completed certain requirements. Most recently, the latter has been both prevalent and controversial. Some missionaries have developed new strategies as they considered the interface of Matthew 28:18–20, Matthew 24:14, and 2 Peter 3:10–12. This need for speed grows out of an interpretation of these passages that the gospel must be preached to every people group, and then Jesus will immediately return. Moreover, many maintain that Jesus cannot return until this happens. In fact, some proponents of this position believe that we are actually hastening the timeline of the return of Christ and the end of the world by our efforts to fulfill the Great Commission. This interpretation sounds solid until one notes the degree to which it implies that God is dependent upon the efforts of humans and the missiological implications that are born of it.

The 1974 Lausanne Conference for World Evangelization was a watershed moment for the way missionaries would think of their target fields for decades to come. As previously mentioned, it was during this conference that Ralph Winter announced that although many thought that the presence of a church in every geopolitical nation around the world meant that the Great Commission was completed, this was far from the truth. He reminded the gathered missionaries, agency heads, and pastors that in the Great Commission Jesus had sent His church to make disciples of all the *people groups*, not merely geopolitical countries. He further reported that his research revealed that of the 24,000 people groups in the world, 10,000 of them were still unreached. The next few years saw mission agencies rethinking their strategies and methodologies in order to incorporate people group thinking. In addition to some incorporating new philosophies and strategies into existing mission agencies, others formed new agencies over the next two decades to facilitate the identification and reaching of every people group in the world. Luis Bush wrote, "Joshua Project 2000 is a strategy that seeks to obey the Great Commission and the commandment of Jesus to His followers by going to 'make disciples of all nations' (Matthew

28:19). Specifically, the goal is to establish, at a minimum, a pioneer church-planting movement among every people (or *ethne*). The church planting movements will fulfill the Lord's call to 'love your neighbor as yourself' (Luke 10:27) and to 'preach good news to the poor . . . to proclaim freedom for the prisoners and recovery of sight for the blind, to release the oppressed' (Luke 4:18)."[25]

In considering the balance between search and harvest theologies, we must understand several pertinent Bible passages that are regularly quoted as conclusive evidence to support the wisdom of a chosen missions strategy. While these passages should certainly inform our understanding of the missionary task, we must not force them out of context to proclaim an extreme that is not present.

Matthew 28:18–20

Jesus has commanded His church to go into all the world and make disciples. While some have taken Jesus' words as exclusively for those who were standing and hearing Him that day, His promise to be with His church to the end of the age as they carried out the command reveals that its extent went beyond them. His command necessarily includes going and preaching the gospel. While some have argued the importance of the fact that *"Go"* is a participle rather than the imperative form of the word in the Great Commission, we cannot drop the idea of *going* from the thrust of the passage.

In addition, Jesus is very clearly commissioning His hearers to make disciples of all the *ethne*, or people groups, of the world; so of course, going is an important part of His command. However, simply going is not enough; what are we to go and do? Jesus makes clear that we are to go, make disciples, and teach them. When we permit the need for speed or clever missiological strategies to reduce the Great Commission to simply "going and reaching and leaving," we fail to obey the words of Christ in His last command to His church. Jesus has commanded His church to go into the entire world and preach the gospel, making disciples in every people group, baptizing them and teaching them to observe all He has commanded us to be and do.

Matthew 24:14

Many modern missionaries and their agencies have made their understanding of Matthew 24:14 the driving force of the missionary task. The context of this passage is Jesus explaining to His disciples what will happen at the end of the age. The disciples have just pointed out to Him the beauty of the temple buildings, and He sobers them with the revelation that this would all be destroyed. He continues by telling them what to look for in the signs of the close of the age. In Matthew 24:14, Jesus says, "And this gospel of the kingdom will be proclaimed throughout the whole world as a testimony to all nations, and then the end will come." Some argue that in this verse Jesus gives us the key to ushering in the kingdom. They believe that in saying that the gospel must be preached to every people group before the end can come, the formula is laid out for bringing Him back. They further believe that Jesus cannot come back until we have accomplished this task, as we understand it. The excitement grows in their argument as they explain that missions researchers have identified every people group on the planet for the first time in history. They have categorized all of these groups as either reached or unreached and have a strategy in place to reach all the unreached and preach the gospel—and then Jesus will immediately return and the end will come.

If they are correct, then certainly everyone should drop what they are doing and join them in reaching and preaching to every people group as quickly as possible. In fact, to the degree that anyone is doing something other than joining this strategy, such as teaching in a pastors' training school, tending orphans, digging wells, or feeding the hungry, they are delaying the coming of the Lord. The need for speed comes into sharp focus as we examine the missionary task in this light. However, as you might suspect, there are some significant problems with this interpretation.

First, Jesus is not here describing the strategy for ushering in the kingdom; He is instead telling the disciples to be patient and endure the persecutions to come; in other words, He is not telling them how to speed up the kingdom but how to await its coming with long-suffering and faithful endurance. He is describing to them the kinds of events that will occur and the state of the world before the end comes. If the disciples had understood Jesus' words to be clues as to what they could do to advance the day of His return, they would have begun a demolition project to make sure no stone remained on another (Matthew 24:2). Moreover, if missiologists consider this verse to be Jesus' instructions for completing our work on earth and bringing Him back, why haven't they been consistent with their logic and devised a strategy for the Jews? Most eschatological views include at least some understanding of what God intends before the end of history for the Jewish people (usually from Romans 9–11). Indeed, many believe that God is not through with the Jews and that there will be a massive awakening among them. Therefore, if missiologists are to be consistent, there should also be a vast recruitment campaign to send missionaries to facilitate the revival among the Jews in Israel, New York, Miami, and wherever they are found.

AS THE DIRECTOR of an intensive semester-long discipleship program for young adults, I encountered many young people with an undeniable passion for God's mission embedded in a fragmented and incoherent vision of the Christian faith. It takes time, commitment, and faithful community to cover naked passion with the full wardrobe of a holistic Christian worldview. More than that, though, it takes the gracious rush of the Holy Spirit to capture our affections and to make us yearn for the beauty of Him who still looks so much like death to us. I believe that the task of mission is not complete until converts are rooted in a Christian community that can nourish and instigate continual growth in the Christian faith.

—DAVID SONJU

Former director of the LIFT Discipleship Program

Second, many commentators debate whether Jesus is referring in Matthew 24:14 to the end of the world and His return or to the end of the Jewish state and Jerusalem. Arguing for the end of the Jewish state, some commentators believe that the words of Jesus were fulfilled in AD 70 when the Romans destroyed the temple. Moreover, following this line of reasoning, they hold that everything necessary for Jesus to return was fulfilled in that first century. For this reason, the New Testament writers could clearly anticipate the return of Christ any day.

There are several views on how we are best to understand Jesus' prophetic teaching in this passage. Is Jesus speaking of events that will precede His second coming or to things that will take place during the lifetime of those to whom He was speaking that day? The biblical context, historical reflection, and language shed light on how we are to understand Jesus' meaning in all of the Olivet Discourse, and particularly in Matthew 24:14. The perspective referred to as the partial preterist view, held by many scholars such as R. C. Sproul, contends that Matthew 24:14, along with the full Olivet Discourse, is speaking primarily of the coming destruction of Jerusalem and the temple that took place in AD 70.

The context of the Olivet Discourse reveals that tensions were high in Jerusalem, and Jesus knew that the establishment would reject Him as Messiah. Additionally, extrabiblical writings confirm the fulfillment of several circumstances Jesus mentions, including those regarding false prophets, wars, and upheavals. Yet, a plain English reading of Matthew 24:14 seems to contradict the partial preterist belief that the events refer to the first century, as the gospel has still not been proclaimed in the "whole world." However, in a study of this passage, R. C. Sproul and Ligonier Ministries made the following observation: "Many do not accept a partial preterist analysis of Matthew 24:1–35 because the 'whole world' has not yet heard the Gospel (v. 14). The Greek word used for 'whole world,' however, is *oikoumene*, or the 'world of the Roman empire.'"[26] While *oikoumene* can also be used to refer to the entire world, the Pauline use in Romans reveals that Paul understood it to refer to the Roman world.

He considered the gospel to have been preached in the *oikoumene* except for Spain, where he would preach before he died. Therefore, according to this view, Matthew 24:14 was fulfilled prior to the death of Paul.[27] The Great Commission commands us to go, and Jesus' words prior to His ascension remind us that we are to do so to the ends of the earth. These commands are met with the promise that some from the whole world will hear and respond, as we see in Revelation 7:9. However, the historical context and the language Jesus used does not allow Matthew 24:14 to be a formula to hasten His return or even a promise for exactly when that will occur.

Third, the modern-day application of this verse to the missionary's task and strategy is problematic for several reasons. The argument is that once we preach to every people group, Jesus will immediately return. However, what is the gospel of the kingdom? What does it mean to proclaim it throughout the whole world to every people group? What is an unreached people group? And, once this is done, when will the end come?

What is the gospel of the kingdom? It is the truth that a person must encounter and embrace to be saved. This message teaches first that God is holy, and as such, He is morally perfect and separated from everything and everyone that is not. Second, the gospel teaches that all men and women are sinful and therefore are unable to approach Him in their own efforts. The good news appears to be bad news until we reach the third point, which is that Jesus is the solution to man's sin problem. He lived a perfectly holy life, died to pay for the sins of those who will believe on Him, and freely grants them the righteousness God requires. The fourth point of the gospel message emphasizes that these truths do not result in the salvation of everyone, but of those who repent of their sins and place faith in Jesus. The gospel of the kingdom is not merely to agree with a set of facts to join a church; it is rather the way to enter into a right relationship with the King.

What does it mean to proclaim the gospel message? The need for speed has driven some agencies to forgo language training for its missionaries, preferring to use national interpreters since the missionaries will be moving on quickly. Unfortunately, many of these interpreters are not believers, and the message they communicate is not the gospel. As countless missionaries can attest, even the best, believing interpreters can unintentionally muddle the message. Such mistakes often go uncorrected and become accepted doctrine. Many missionaries try to learn the language and strive to communicate the gospel clearly, but cultural baggage from tribal legends, myths, worldview differences, and intercultural communication challenges can hinder adequate proclamation of the true gospel for years.

Additionally, is our modern-day understanding of people groups or nations the same definition that Jesus had in mind? Beginning in 1974, the US Center for World Mission estimated that there were 24,000 people groups in the world; this number represented the 10,000 unreached groups and the 14,000 reached groups.[28] After further research, the USCWM has since revised this to 27,000 people groups, with 13,000 being unreached and 14,000 reached.[29] The International Mission Board calculates that there are 11,601 people groups with 6,426 of them being unreached.[30] Joshua Project's research believes that there are 16,367 people groups with 6,645 being unreached.[31] We have already established that there are various ways of counting people groups, and there are different criteria for determining which groups are unreached. But we must ask whether Jesus' way of considering the people groups of the world is the same as ours. Moreover, what is an unreached group? There are a variety of ways to measure whether a group is reached, but more to the point, when may it be said that the gospel of the kingdom has been preached to a people group sufficiently so that we may push on to the next one?

Does Matthew 24:14 say that Jesus will return immediately? Given the hope that we find in such an interpretation, it is tempting to embrace it and press on to preach the gospel to every group as quickly as possible. However, Jesus does not actually say that the end will come immediately. Given the doctrinally unsound state of the church around the world where the need for speed has led missionaries to preach a simple gospel message through an interpreter, get a show of hands, call them a church, and move on, we should shudder to consider what the church would be like at the end of such a missions strategy. What would become of the church should Jesus delay His return for fifty years? Or, five hundred years? How many heresies would creep into an untaught church? How many cults would have descended on the new believers to reap the harvest?

2 Peter 3:10–12

Some missionaries appeal to this passage in Peter's second letter and add "hastening the end of the world" to the missionary task. "But the day of the Lord will come like a thief, and then the heavens will pass away with a roar, and the heavenly bodies will be burned up and dissolved, and the earth and the works that are done on it will be exposed. Since all these things are thus to be dissolved, what sort of people ought you to be in lives of holiness and godliness, waiting for and hastening the coming of the day of God, because of which the heavens will be set on fire and dissolved, and the heavenly bodies will melt as they burn!" (2 Peter 3:10–12).

The context of the passage is that believers should not be afraid of the end of the world but rather anticipate it. We should not drag about in dread of the coming day but live holy lives that are pleasing to God and strive to make our lives count for the advance of His kingdom. In so doing, we are fulfilling what God has ordained for us for the culmination of all things. A sense of urgency should accompany missionaries in their efforts, and they should never adopt a casual attitude about communicating the gospel to lost sinners, who are hopeless without it. However, the God of the Bible is not a wondering Deity who is wringing His hands and waiting for humans to decide the calendar date of the culmination of His plan. God already knows the day of Christ's return and the end of the world (Matthew 24:36; Acts 17:31) and while Christians have a role to play, it is not one of speeding up the day in the timeline of God's plan.

CONCLUSION

The basic arguments of whether it is better to search for unreached people groups or bring in the harvest among responsive people groups should be considered in light of the fact that both are biblical, both glorify God, and both advance His kingdom. Missionaries who are seeking the best investment of their lives should remember that the highest and best use of anyone's life is to do exactly what God calls them to do in the places He calls them to do it.

There is no arbitrary percentage point to determine when missionary work is over in a particular area or people group. God is the one who determines the times of our lives and the exact places where we should live (Acts 17:26), and He works out all things in conformity with the purpose of His will (Ephesians 1:11). When missionaries base their coming and going on such arbitrary percentages, they often overlook the truth that His ways and thoughts are not ours (Isaiah 55:9).

(After all, the best way to make an unreached people group is to abandon one that is reached.) The churches of Europe were the sending churches of the missionaries who brought and established Christianity in the United States. The church in the USA joined Europe in sending missionaries all over the world. Today, researchers employing the 2 percent criterion to define the unreached must declare Europe to be unreached.

Yes, the unreached search fields much be reached with the saving gospel message. However, the harvest fields must have discipled evangelists, trained pastors, theologically educated teachers, and biblically sound churches. May God bless the missiological and ethnographic research that dedicated men and women are amassing for missions advance, but may missionaries seek to know where God is leading them and be faithful to that call—no matter where.

Suggested Reading

Blackaby, Henry. *Experiencing God: Knowing and Doing the Will of God*. Nashville: B&H Books, 2008.

Bush, Luis. "What Is Joshua Project 2000?" *Mission Frontiers* 17 (November/December 1995).

Cronk, Jarod. "Joshua Project Step 6: Planting Churches in Each of These Peoples," *Mission Frontiers* 17 (November/December 1995).

Engel, James F. "Beyond the Numbers Game," *Christianity Today*, August 7, 2000.

Engel, James F. and William A. Dyrness. *Changing the Mind of Missions: Where Have We Gone Wrong?* Downers Grove, IL: InterVarsity Press, 2000.

Hesselgrave, David J. *Paradigms in Conflict: 10 Key Questions in Christian Missions Today*. Grand Rapids: Kregel, 2006.

McGavran, Donald. *Understanding Church Growth*. 3rd ed. Edited by C. Peter Wagner. Grand Rapids: Eerdmans, 1990.

Piper, John. *Let the Nations Be Glad!* 2nd ed. Grand Rapids: Baker Academic, 2003.

Scribner, Dan. "Joshua Project Step 1: Identifying the Peoples Where Church Planting Is Most Needed," *Mission Frontiers* 17 (November/December 1995).

Wagner, C. Peter. "On the Cutting Edge." In *Perspectives on the World Christian Movement*, edited by Ralph Winter, 531–40. Pasadena, CA; William Carey Library, 1999.

Walker, Alan. *A Ringing Call to Mission*. New York: Abingdon Press, 1966.

7

TECHNIQUES AND TOOLS: THE GREATER GOOD, CPM, AND WHAT ONLY GOD CAN DO

The belief that human manipulation can force God's hand and bring about divine blessing has resulted in many of the problems that we have seen thus far. I suggest that we consider this belief misguided rather than sinful. The proponents of such thinking no doubt love the Lord, long to see His kingdom advanced in the world, and have pure motivations. However, faulty hermeneutics, a low view of Scripture, inadequate biblical foundations, or a lack of theological education among many of those who employ these methods cause syncretism, heresy, and weak churches around the world. Many poorly equipped new missionaries who learn about these suggested methods for reaching the world and embrace them as the best techniques are unable to balance them with the teachings of the whole counsel of the Word of God.

Techniques and tools do not require end users to share the world-view of their inventors. The worker using a hammer to drive a nail does not need to know or care about the politics and religious views of the person who made it. The inventor could be wise and godly and the worker could be the opposite. Additionally, people often use tools for purposes that the inventors never intended. No one ever designed and built a car for a drunk driver to get home from a bar or for use as a bank robbery getaway vehicle. Tragically, inexperienced teen-aged drivers sometimes drive in ways that the car designer, road builder, and gasoline provider never intended. The result is that people get hurt. Similarly, missiological techniques and tools designed or envisioned by sincere missionaries with godly purposes in mind are often used in ways they never intended. It is this misuse and abuse of what could be sound methodologies that we must critique and denounce, not the sincere missionaries who are so often behind them.

When faced with the challenge of reaching all of the people groups in the world as quickly as possible, missiologists and strategists employ every tool available to accomplish the task. Humans do not deal well with a vacuum; we want to fill the void, finish the job, or find the solution to every problem. This is especially true among Westerners with our modern worldview. Give us a calculator, a laboratory, and enough time, and we believe that we can solve any problem. This mentality has also sought to address the spiritual needs of lost mankind around the world. It is common for a solution that worked in one place to be suggested and become the flavor-of-the-month employed everywhere. The result is often that missionaries with wildly varying ethical systems or theological stances utilize it with their own spin and expression. Even when they use methods that are biblically or ethically questionable, some missionaries defend the practice, all in the name of the greater good.

THE GREATER GOOD MENTALITY

The greater good mentality saturates and drives much of the thinking in missions today. This mentality is one way to define the view that the ends justify the means. For instance, a desired end that is best for a people is sometimes sought through unethical means as long as the effort is successful and the goal is attained. A few years ago, a Latin American country considered the indigenous population to be growing too quickly and hurting the overall population by their sheer numbers and "backward" ways. Government officials allegedly enforced a sterilization program for the indigenous women, justifying it as "best" for the people group and the nation. The same kind of logic leads even godly missionaries who are seeking to achieve biblical ends to embrace this greater good mentality and employ questionable means to obtain desired results.

The clear command of Christ is to reach and teach the peoples of the world. With such a clear goal, missionaries strategize to accomplish it. Finding that certain countries will not allow them to enter as missionaries, they must seek other ways to enter and fulfill the Great Commission there. At other times, their own agencies demand doctrinal or procedural guidelines that the missionaries do not share, and they struggle with how to do what God called them to do. There may also be pressure from supporters, supervisors, or the sense of "shoulds-and-oughts" that leads many missionaries to do whatever is necessary to get the decisions from the nationals. In agencies that place great emphasis on church planting, the pressure to perform may cause the missionary or agency to redefine what a church is in order to obtain greater numbers of new churches. Let's consider each of these scenarios with a greater good mentality.

Creative Access Platforms

Missionaries have worked in gospel-hostile areas throughout history. Yet gaining access to these countries is often challenging. Some governments will not allow missionaries to enter on a missionary visa, and others actively seek to identify and limit Christian Westerners through the visa application process. In the countries that do not allow a missionary visa, Christian workers must seek entrance on other platforms such as English teachers, business consultants, or tour agency operators. The visa that they obtain allows them to serve in their stated capacities while also developing relationships, sharing the gospel, discipling new believers, and planting churches. While the end of the Cold War brought about greater initial access to many countries, a recent tightening of these freedoms reminds missionaries of the wisdom of utilizing legitimate platforms in case the door closes to missionaries.

Christians unfamiliar with the creative access approach may struggle with the ethics involved. After all, the Bible commands Christians to be the best citizens in the land, to be obedient, and to respect the leaders and governments God has established (Romans 13:1–7; 1 Peter 2:13–17). However, we also read of the apostles telling governing authorities that they must obey God rather than man (Acts 5:29). Moreover, God has commanded us to go and make disciples of all nations (Matthew 28:18–20). Clearly, there is a balance; but what is it? Must believers always tell the truth, the whole truth, and nothing but the truth?

An old adage says, "All's fair in love and war." We see an example of this in Joshua 2 where Rahab lies to protect the Hebrew spies and is rewarded for it. In fact, she is even mentioned in Hebrews 11's "Hall of Faith." There are times when armies lie and send misinformation to the enemy about a frontal attack, only to move quickly to new positions and attack the enemy's flank. Such deception may spare countless lives, and we reward the officers for their wise strategy. In sports, a player will feint in one direction and run another, and no one considers this to be a sin or calls the player to repent. Likewise, since we live in a fallen world, many Christian missionaries consider the spiritual warfare they face as a result of kingdom work to be justification for lying to the government in the countries where they work.

Mission agencies that employ creative access strategies and platforms teach their missionaries to devise a short tenable statement that they can present to immigration officials or inquiring neighbors. A missionary entering a creative access country may obtain a student visa to study the national language in a university setting where she hopes to win and disciple students. In this case, her short tenable statement would be: "I am a student living here and attending the university to study your national language." Her difficulty is when friends ask how she is able to study full time and not have to work. Where does her money come from? Why did she come to this country? Does she work for some company that sent her? Prying questions eventually arrive at the point where a short tenable statement will not suffice. Is she to lie to protect her "cover"?

One of the thorny issues to resolve is what to say when the nationals—even new believers among them—eventually find out. On the surface, it seems easy enough. The missionary may reason that the national will be a believer by then and will certainly understand and support the reasons for lying. However, missionaries are learning that it is not always so easy. Many young believers feel betrayed and wonder what else the missionary has lied about. Indeed, some have turned away from the missionary and his or her Christ as unethical, believing that whatever else it is, Christianity is assuredly not what they thought it was.

In addition to the access they gain, some missionaries are attracted to the excitement of living and working on creative access platforms that require security procedures as if they were international secret agents. Indeed, some agencies have unexpectedly found success recruiting missionary candidates with this unique missionary career. Countless young people want to be on the cutting edge and imagine themselves as a James Bond, Jason Bourne, or Jack Bauer for Jesus. However, this trendy and exciting element of creative access ministries often results in many missionaries maintaining the façade even when it is not necessary. Thinking through every visa application, daily encounter, and ministry opportunity, then weighing the tension of telling the truth with the stewardship of continued freedom to live in the country eventually takes its toll. When missionaries tire of the tension of seeking the balance and decide to maintain the cover for cover's sake, their credibility, their integrity, and the gospel suffer. Some missionaries become accustomed to misrepresentation of facts even without needing to, because lies are not necessarily a negative factor in the greater good mentality. Some reason, "If a lie will work to keep me here or bring people to Jesus, then the end justifies the means." It is draining to maintain truth in a setting that requires creative access, so the greater good mentality devises a short tenable statement of truth that will suffice.

Doctrinal Positions and Operating Procedures

A few years ago, a mission agency adopted a new version of its doctrinal statement. This statement was not a major shift, and indeed most missionaries felt that it was not a significant change from what they originally understood to be the agency's stance. The agency required all new missionary candidates to sign the statement certifying their acceptance and adherence, and all deployed field missionaries also had to either sign it or resign their positions. After considering it, many immediately signed the statement without qualms, but others interpreted it as a major shift and did not agree with it. They knew that the ones who provided their support—and to whom they had submitted themselves—were requiring something they could not agree to, so they resigned with broken hearts and returned to the USA. However, many others reasoned with the greater good mentality, believing that God called them to serve where they were, and if signing a piece of paper allowed them to stay and continue doing it—whether they agreed with it and intended to live by it or not—they would sign it and continue to minister.

Lying to a pagan government in order to gain access and spread the gospel is one thing, but it is quite another to lie to your own agency or denomination, which provides your salary or visa and sends you out to do missions under their auspices. However, the greater good mentality allows them to justify conveniently and easily such subterfuge for the advance of the gospel . . . or at least for a career that purports to do so.

Missiological Methods

Sometimes students and would-be missionary candidates ask the question, "What do missionaries do all day long?" Of course, the answer depends on the missionary. Every team or missionary has a style, technique, or preferred approach to missions. Some arriving missionaries are finding procedures in place that range from the novel to the heretical. For instance, missionaries going to work in Muslim contexts may find it odd that the missionaries use Allah for the name of God. Although Christians used the name Allah to refer to God for centuries before the birth of Mohammed, today many Christians and Muslims alike struggle with the legitimacy of this practice as Allah is now clearly understood to be the name for the Muslim god. Indeed, at least one Muslim country has outlawed the use of Allah by Christians to refer to their God.

A controversial evangelism technique, the Camel Method, evangelizes Muslims by utilizing passages of the Quran that speak of Jesus. While the Quran does speak of the historical person of Jesus and attributes to Him admirable qualities, missionaries must remember that Muslims are very familiar with the Quran and this passage about Jesus and are not likely to be automatically swayed by it, as if they have never considered it. Additionally, the Quran also teaches many false and heretical things about the person of Jesus. Missionaries should be careful about using the Quran as an evangelism tool if all they know about it is Surah Al-Imran 3:42–55, the passage from the Quran that the Camel Method utilizes. This would be tantamount to a Muslim who is only familiar with one Old Testament chapter trying to use it to evangelize a Christian Bible scholar. While in certain circumstances the use of the Quran could provide a bridge across which the evangelist may lead a Muslim to the gospel, many feel that this method legitimizes the Quran in the mind of the Muslim. In fact, missionaries have seen that when Muslims come to the Lord through this use of the Quran, they often continue to use the Quran for years and value it as a Christian's holy book alongside the Bible.[1]

Another controversial aspect of ministry among Muslims relates to the gospel-hostile contexts where they often live. Because of the danger to Muslims who convert to Christianity, some missionaries encourage them to change little or nothing about their lives when they become Christians. New Muslim-background Christians often continue going to the mosque, reading the Quran, praying toward Mecca five times a day, and even daily repeating the *shahada:* "I bear witness that there is no God but Allah and that Muhammad is His servant and messenger."

Additionally, other missionaries in these areas introduce themselves as Muslims since the word simply means "one who submits." They reason that, after all, they submit to God. However, virtually every hearer of the word "Muslim" understands it to mean "one who submits to Allah according to the teachings of the prophet Mohammed." Where is the missionary's angst, tension, or struggle for balance in all of this? Increasingly, the greater good mentality erases the tension. If using these techniques results in the missionary's ability to stay in the country, stay safe, and get people to pray a prayer, many believe that there is no problem. The end justifies the means.

No doubt, certain aspects of all of these arguments have great merit in some instances. Missionaries often argue that when the target culture context is so hostile, pagan, or brainwashed, missiological tools and methodologies must be unorthodox to be effective. Then how much stronger is the argument that in these places, of all places, missionaries should disciple believers and teach the Scriptures and theology to present everyone mature in Christ Jesus?

In an animistic context of Southeast Asia, some missionaries considered focusing their evangelistic presentations on the animists' fear of spirits, ghosts, magic, and powerful forces. In line with this focus, they debated a strategy of telling these animistic peoples how Jesus would come to live in them if they accepted Him, and that His Spirit is more powerful than the spirits of the world. This would have been very effective to get people to flock to the churches, but the problem is that they would have brought their sin with them. Someone wisely counseled these missionaries that it is our sin that separates us from God, not our fear. Evangelists must confront their hearers about sin and call them to repent and believe, and the confrontation must be ethical and presented with integrity.

Some missionary evangelists have gone way beyond these techniques and embraced methods that are deceitful or considered trickery. Webster's online dictionary defines a charlatan as "a flamboyant deceiver; one who attracts customers with tricks or jokes."[2] Sadly, we could apply this to some missionaries. I recently heard of one who would trick people into praying a sinner's prayer by feigning poor eyesight and asking them to read the tract aloud. Their "readers" may have vocalized the words in the prayer, but were no more saved than they were before the encounter with the missionary and praying the prayer. Others have used terror tactics to manipulate children by frightening them with the horrors of hell to get them to raise a hand to avoid the flames. Unfortunately, these children never learned anything about sin, Jesus, or the gospel. For those who believe that merely reciting a prayer brings salvation, the method for getting them to do so apparently is of little consequence when ministering in the name of the greater good.

Our great missionary example, the apostle Paul, wrote, "But we have renounced disgraceful, underhanded ways. We refuse to practice cunning or to tamper with God's word, but by the open statement of the truth we would commend ourselves to everyone's conscience in the sight of God" (2 Corinthians 4:2). How many of the shameful methods and tactics utilized in missions and evangelism today would fall by the wayside if we practiced the missiological methods of Paul and returned to the Bible as our only rule of faith and practice? Paul also speaks to the argument for diminishing overt Christian witness to avoid persecution in gospel-hostile places:

> *We put no obstacle in anyone's way, so that no fault may be found with our ministry, but as servants of God we commend ourselves in every way: by great endurance, in afflictions, hardships, calamities, beatings, imprisonments, riots, labors, sleepless nights, hunger; by purity, knowledge, patience, kindness, the Holy Spirit, genuine love; by truthful speech, and the power of God; with the weapons of righteousness for the right hand and for the left; through honor and dishonor, through slander and praise. We are treated as impostors, and yet are true; as unknown, and yet well known; as dying, and behold, we live; as punished, and yet not killed; as sorrowful, yet always rejoicing; as poor, yet making many rich; as having nothing, yet possessing everything.* (2 Corinthians 6:3–10)

Notice especially verse 7, "By truthful speech, and the power of God; with the weapons of righteousness for the right hand and for the left." Missionaries are to speak the truth, being as wise as serpents but as harmless as doves, trusting God for protection when He so wills to grant it. The problem with the greater good mentality is that men and women are the ones defining the desired "good" instead of God, who alone is wise.

The Bible never divorces the concepts of evangelism and discipleship as many do in our day. A holistic, biblical ministry incorporates both as two sides of a single coin. The greater good mentality in evangelism means taking the path of least resistance and using whatever method results in the most measurable decisions as quickly as possible.

WITHOUT REALIZING IT, our Western concern for speed and numbers has led to evangelism which results in churches. Who can argue with such a noble goal as this? However, there is something unsettling implied in this type of approach. The newly evangelized are immediately propelled into church leadership positions. There is no other alternative. An extreme example of this is a well-meaning international volunteer organization, which endeavored to start five churches in four days. There was a leap from evangelism to church leadership without passing through the slow and intentional discipleship process. An additional challenge is the non-biblical nature of the existing church. Thus, if new believers gather for "church" too quickly, their own non-biblical model of a church will automatically be imposed on the new church plant. The only remedy for this seems to be a careful slow discipleship process, which allows believers to discover "church" in the Bible and then implement what they have discovered.

—STAN WAFLER

Missionary, Northwest Uganda

Ecclesiology

When the pressure is on to produce the greatest number of churches, missionaries often choose techniques that result in the most churches in the least amount of time. However, because there is no quick shortcut to producing New Testament churches with biblically qualified leaders, the definition of what a church is becomes adjustable to the current reality. Some missionaries consider a group that agrees to meet weekly for prayer, Bible study, and fellowship to be a new church. Other missionaries will consider a new church to be a home where someone agrees to host a Bible study. One team of church planting missionaries defended such loose ecclesiology with, "It's just like Jesus said, 'Where two or more are gathered in my name, there is my church.'" But this is not what Jesus said; He merely promised His *presence* in such a setting (Matthew 18:20).

Other missionaries seek to start as many churches as possible, but they want the churches to be biblically sound. They understand that new churches reach more people faster and tend to welcome new people into their fellowship more readily. New believers can use existing friendships and family relationships to facilitate church planting more quickly. Missionaries Tim and Rebecca Lewis wrote of utilizing these natural relationships in church planting: "In each case, they were welcomed into a cohesive community, so the Gospel was shared with the whole group. As a result, people already committed to each other came to faith together. A church was born within a natural community, without creating a new group just for fellowship. It reminded us of something Ralph Winter has said, 'The "church" (i.e., committed community) is already there, they just don't know Jesus yet!'"[3] It is easy to see how others with a greater good mentality could take the Lewises' model and use it as license to redefine the church and church planting. Many missionaries burdened by the need for speed and freed by the greater good mentality have jettisoned the 1 Timothy 3:1–7 qualifications for pastors. In ever-increasing ways, the definition of a church, the qualifications of church leaders, and the mission agency's position on these matters are all subservient to the greater good.

THE CURRENT WIND of missionary thinking is that if we focus on mobilizing and training of nationals to plant churches, then the nationals will teach themselves. In practice, teaching, training, and mentoring of leaders are not default tasks; thus we cannot assume that they will automatically do it, especially if someone does not model it. Paul exhorted Timothy to focus on the teaching of leaders, showing that teaching may not have been a default reaction of evangelization as we currently expect from nationals (2 Timothy 2:2). Any movement of planting churches or multiplying churches requires the theological and ministry formation of leaders.

—DAVID BLEDSOE
Urban evangelist and church planting trainer, Brazil

CHURCH PLANTING MOVEMENTS

One of the last decade's most prolific methodologies is Church Planting Movements (CPM). To be fair to the other strategies and methodologies that missionaries employed in the same period, CPM became one of the most prolific because the largest mission agency mandated its use as the golden-key, single-solution strategy for all of its missionaries worldwide. While the proponents of CPMs argue that it is not a methodology, when this agency insisted on it as their global *modus operandi* it became a de facto methodology. The chief architect of the movement defined CPM this way: "A Church Planting Movement is a rapid multiplication of indigenous churches planting churches that sweeps through a people group or population segment."[4] He believes that CPM is the way to finish the Great Commission task as fast as possible. Drawing from Madeleine L'Engle's *A Wrinkle in Time*, he asks, "What is the shortest distance between two points?" and answers that it is not a line but a wrinkle.[5] CPM seeks to multiply rapidly by planting churches that plant churches that plant churches. In order for this to happen, the old linear method of winning people to Christ one by one, then discipling them, then leading a Bible study, and then becoming a church, and so on, must be set aside as too slow. CPM emphasizes "wrinkling" the line and doing all the steps at once, rather than doing one step at a time, and then instilling this paradigm in the DNA of the new churches.

Proponents of CPM and similar strategies for church planting appeal to Luke 10:1–12 as their biblical basis and model. However, Luke 10:1–12 has nothing to do with church planting but rather relates a time when Jesus sent His apostles out on a short-term evangelistic trip. Indeed, many argue that the church was not even born until the day of Pentecost when the Holy Spirit was poured out to live in believers.

Other mission agencies have adopted similar approaches to plant churches as quickly as possible in the fields where they work. For instance, Short-Cycle Church Planting (SCCP) has been described as a strategy "to develop mature, reproducing churches led by nationals within five years of arrival in the field. . . . With this approach, every element of the church planting process, from language learning to evangelism to leadership development, is *undertaken simultaneously* and accomplished *as efficiently as possible* within our faith context. . . . [T]he goal is to establish and develop a church *as quickly as possible.*" Indeed, SCCP's own way of wrinkling time to satisfy the need for speed is termed "*Simultaneous Activity*—Instead of thinking sequentially, the team will focus on all phases of church planting *concurrently.*" Like the CPM emphasis on widespread seed-sowing and identifying the person of peace in each community, the SCCP model calls for the team to "*sow the seed of the gospel early, often and directly* with a view to *finding key people* who will fully evangelize their community." Additionally, as CPM aims to avoid dependency and begins the race with the baton already in the hands of the nationals (rather than passing it off at some point in the future), so does SCCP: "We strive to *eliminate dependency* by involving nationals *at all levels* of ministry." SCCP does not veil the need for speed. "The team will continuously look for leverage that will *accelerate* their efforts" (all emphases added).[6] Given the detailed similarities of such rapid church planting strategies, I refer to them all with the term CPM in this chapter.

In his critique of CPM methodology, Hoyt Lovelace stressed the culture clash that this paradigm often brings in addition to inadequate attention that "wrinkling time" gives to discipleship and teaching. "For many reasons the amount of stress placed on wrinkling time and rapidity of explosive growth can betray the final goal and result in the appearance of impatience and lack of care in some social structures."[7] Lovelace points out that CPMs do in fact seek to place local leaders in ministry positions, but without the essential training that they need. Lovelace explained, "A key defining point of CPM methodology rests in the description of leadership within the movement. Local leadership is of primary importance as it has been observed that the strongest CPMs tend to be those with the least amount of foreign involvement. For this reason, CPM practitioners develop local leaders and entrust to them the future of the movement as quickly as possible."[8] However, as we have seen, the need for speed moves the timeline up much faster than is healthy for the churches that will remain behind. Appointing elders in every church and utilizing local leadership is biblical and wise. However, they must be biblically qualified, God-called, and trained leaders if the missionaries are faithful to the Scriptures.

Developing these elements in the leaders may slow the work and the advance into new areas. Anything that slows the work is an undesirable impediment to the greater good. When the greater good mentality unites with CPM methodology, a powerful force is unleashed. The power of this union provides the speed that many missionaries think they need.

This speed requires the missionary to cut corners and eliminate peripherals. Anyone who stands in the way or pushes back is seen to be, at best, not a team player, and at worst, hindering the advance of the gospel. This discussion is not an exposé about the reported

CPMs that have been weighed and found wanting. Others have written to expose CPMs whose numbers were inflated, or where nationals were paid to maintain ministries and give the appearance of a CPM, or to reveal the fact that most reported CPMs crumble when examined closely. In fact, the few CPMs that survive under bright lights contain many exceptions to the prescribed strategy/methodology that the missionaries are to follow.

Standing in Buenos Aires, looking down a seemingly endless boulevard with high-rise apartment buildings on both sides, I was challenged by a young missionary who was employing CPM methodology in that city to consider the great need to locate a church in every one of those buildings. He recounted all their efforts and how they are just scratching the surface with many but are trying to move on quickly to cover as much ground as possible. It was obvious that his burdened heart wanted to race from building to building to fulfill the Great Commission. He asked me how I thought they could do a better job. I replied, "Slow down."

WHAT ONLY GOD CAN DO

Charles Finney was one whom God had burdened for lost souls and called to preach the gospel. In his zeal, he sought to devise ways to assist churches to experience revival. He studied the revivals and awakenings of history and concluded that the following earmarks characterize the churches that experience them.

1. When the providence of God indicates that a revival is at hand. The indications of God's providence are sometimes so plain as to amount to a revelation of His will. There is a conspiring of events to open the way, a preparation of circumstances to favor a revival, so that those who are looking out can see that a revival is at hand, just as plainly as if it had been revealed from heaven.
2. When the wickedness of the wicked grieves and humbles and distresses Christians.

3. A revival may be expected when Christians have a spirit of prayer for a revival. That is, when they pray as if their hearts were set upon a revival.
4. Another sign that a revival may be expected, is when the attention of ministers is especially directed to this particular object, and when their preaching and other efforts are aimed particularly for the conversion of sinners.
5. A revival of religion may be expected when Christians begin to confess their sins to one another.
6. A revival may be expected whenever Christians are found willing to make the sacrifice necessary to carry it on.
7. A revival may be expected when ministers and professors are willing to have God promote it by what instruments He pleases.[9]

Finney went beyond merely recognizing the characteristics present in revivals to prescribing steps that ministers may take to ensure them. He believed that ministers could manipulate a revival. Finney wrote, "As I explained last week, the connection between the right use of means for a revival, and a revival, is as philosophically sure as between the right use of means to raise grain, and a crop of wheat. I believe, in fact, it is more certain, and that there are fewer instances of failure. The effect is more certain to follow."[10] Finney continued in his argument, "Do you wish for a revival? Will you have one? If God should ask you this moment by an audible voice from heaven. 'Do you want a revival?' would you dare to say, Yes? 'Are you willing to make the sacrifices?' would you answer, Yes?"[11] Finney concluded, "You see why you have not a revival. It is only because you don't want one. Because you are not praying for it, nor anxious for it, nor putting forth efforts for it."[12] Finney believed that revivals and awakenings were ours for the making. If a pastor wanted a revival, he needed only to follow the prescribed method for ensuring that the required characteristics were present, and God was honor-bound to send it. Jonathan Edwards disagreed, albeit a century before Finney, and had written at length about this issue. Edwards wrote of the temptation toward and the danger of such man-centered manipulation.

During the awakening of 1734–35 Edwards faithfully pursued his pastoral work with reverent wonder, for as already noted, his surprise was genuine. But when he gave his narrative to the world, the simple fact is that no revival could ever be a surprise again. His account showed plainly what kind of preaching would awaken sleepy sinners and what sort of responses could be expected. The day would come too soon when overzealous evangelists would attempt to manipulate audiences so as to elicit the responses described by Edwards, and the revival—if it came—would be not a surprising work of God but a planned contrivance of man.[13]

CPMs are the ecclesiastical, or more precisely, the church planting equivalent of an awakening or revival. Spiritual renewal typically refers to that which occurs within the heart of a believer; revival is that which occurs at the church level. In other words, revival revives those who are alive but lukewarm, and awakening refers to salvation coming to those in the wider area or region—saving those who were formerly spiritually dead. While at any of these levels, the sovereignty of God and the responsibility of man have debatable degrees of involvement, it is God who must begin this work or it will never occur (John 6:44; Ephesians 2:1–10; Philippians 1:6). Human beings may prepare the way, but the work of God may not be either forced or thwarted. A bestselling business book entitled *The Tipping Point* became popular among many missions administrators as a way to make church planting as popular as modern fads so as to induce a CPM. However, missionaries have learned that you cannot force a spiritual "tipping point."

Even the International Mission Board, the agency that devised the CPM approach and implemented it more than any other, has admitted, "The IMB leadership rightly acknowledges that no rapid reproduction of churches can be contrived or manipulated by human ingenuity or programming. An explosive eruption of legitimate churches is the work of the Holy Spirit; but often takes years of patient planting until a rich harvest is reaped."[14] Seeking to develop a culture and ethos of CPM among the missionary force might seem to be a legitimate application of models used in the business world, but it often results in great discouragement and depression when it expects missionaries to do what only God can do. In an article that addresses CPMs and their effectiveness, Gerald Harris reported, "One missionary who viewed the CPM with a cautious eye said, 'Missionaries not experiencing the rapid reproduction of churches get discouraged. This methodology sets up 99 percent of missionaries for certain failure, because if no CPM occurs, most missionaries feel as though they have failed.'"[15]

As the discouragement factor crept up in the IMB, pastoral mission administrators stepped in to counter the blow to hardworking missionaries. Longtime missionary and administrator with the IMB, Clyde Meador, wrote a pastoral letter to encourage missionaries who had not experienced a CPM. He wrote,

> We who are missions leaders have talked so much about CPMs that sometimes we have caused missionaries who are not in the midst of a CPM to feel that they are second-class missionaries, or that they are not adequately carrying out their responsibilities. Yet certainly, the great majority of missionaries—probably 98 percent or more—are not yet experiencing a CPM among the population whom they are seeking to reach. For instance, the missionaries of the International Mission Board are working among 1,200 people groups. Yet, there are fewer than thirty ongoing church planting movements among those people groups. [The great majority of our] missionaries are living on the left side of the graph.[16]

Meador continued, "Our experience is that most CPMs take a long period of cultivation, of relationship development, and credibility building before the harvest time for that people group comes."[17] Indeed, the pages of history are replete with the biographies of missionaries like David Brainerd, William Carey, and Adoniram Judson who worked faithfully for many years without much measurable fruit. Meador concluded wisely,

No personnel can bring about a church planting movement. It is God who moves in the hearts of men and women to respond to Him. It is He who gives the increase. While we can, and must, seek to carry out those best practices that have been demonstrated to best prepare the way for a church planting movement, and we can, and must, avoid those practices that have been demonstrated to hinder the development and continuation of a church planting movement, God is the One who brings about a CPM. As followers of Christ, we must be faithful and obedient to carry out our part in the watering and planting. We must trust that the Lord will use that faithfulness as He brings people to Himself.[18]

As it is not fair to heap blame on missionaries who fail to produce a CPM in their ministries, neither is it right to heap praise on a missionary who experiences one. There are time-proven methods for conducting mission work that are in perfect harmony with scriptural guidelines. Invoking and inviting God's blessing and favor on our mission efforts requires that we work in the way that honors Him: "Those who honor me I will honor" (1 Samuel 2:30). As stated previously, a caution to the greater good mentality certainly would be that while we should be as wise as serpents, we must also be as harmless as doves if we would work in Jesus' name and for His glory.

The great missionary and founder of China Inland Mission, J. Hudson Taylor, said, "God's work done God's way will never lack for God's provision." Many missionaries and their agencies have left harvest fields through the years to follow the direction of their financial supporters' and candidates' interest. However, the Bible should be our guide rather than available resources or the winds of opinion. The late Ralph Winter wrote in 2009, "The last two Mission Handbooks (about five years apart) indicate that church planting missions have grown 2.7% but that relief and development missions have grown 75%. This is 27 times as fast a growth, when the latter were already bigger! If this is not a trend worth analyzing and critiquing I don't know what is. And that is what I am trying to do.

Let's not close our eyes. It is not entirely a good trend and could become far worse."[19] Certainly mission agencies and support-raising missionaries must be sensitive to the preferences of constituents. However, they must stop short of following the trends when they lead out of God's clearly revealed will in the biblical model, definition, and command of missions.

CONCLUSION

Unquestioningly following the trends of popularity and having an uncritical embrace of the need for speed can lead missionaries to revere "whatever works" pragmatism. Many missions strategists are discouraging theological education among missionaries and nationals, saying that training them will slow down the work of Matthew 24:14 and their hopes for rapid advance that utilizes methods such as CPM. They believe that worldwide CPM efforts could reach all the unreached people groups of the world in this generation, which would not merely enable but hasten the return of Christ, thereby rendering all training unnecessary—after all, we will all then be in heaven and not need training. The result is that some modern missiological methodologies so focus on short-term gains that sustained fruit of sound churches and disciples through the ages is an afterthought at best and is often considered unnecessary. A comparison of CPMs and historical awakenings reveals many commonalities; and as no one can force God's hand in an awakening, so no one can force a CPM into existence. We may set the sail, but only the Lord can make the wind blow.

Building on a shaky foundation does not render the solid superstructure we desire. Missionaries should return to the Bible and sound theology to ask how awakenings happen. Who determines when and where the Holy Spirit will pour Himself out on a people? If one believes that this is the will of God in every place, why then doesn't He do so all the time? Doesn't God want the whole world to experience great awakenings all the time? CPM thinking would answer "yes" and conclude that the reason must be something that missionaries can change to enable the awakening or CPM. However, a closer examination of the Bible reveals that God has a sovereign plan. Romans 9:11 speaks of God choosing Jacob from Isaac and Rebekah's twins: "Though they were not yet born and had done nothing either good or bad—in order that God's purpose of election might continue, not because of works but because of his call." The Bible also teaches that nothing inherent in the Jewish nation caused God to choose them. Moreover, in the story of the Israelites' exodus from Egypt, it was God who hardened Pharaoh's heart, having raised him up for the express purpose of glorifying Himself.

Even so, we know from the argument of William Carey's *Enquiry into the Obligations of Christians to Use Means for the Conversion of the Heathen* that God has chosen to use means, and we are those means. Therefore, missionaries should certainly not minister in a way that would hinder a CPM or a Great Awakening; rather, missionaries should definitely work in ways that would facilitate them. However, Jesus did not command His church to go plant churches—even biblically sound ones; He commanded us to make disciples and teach them to observe all that He has commanded. Certainly, planting churches is a natural part of the process, but the emphasis is on making disciples and teaching them.

The greater good mentality leads many into strategies, platforms, paradigms, and methodologies that they admit may not be the most honoring to the Lord. However, they argue that this is necessary when ministering in a fallen world. While Christian missionaries in gospel hostile areas must be careful and wise, they must never lose the tension of weighing truth against the greater good. Years ago, Charles Sheldon wrote a book called *In His Steps*, which gave rise to the question and movement "What Would Jesus Do?" The book recounts the lives of Christians who lived their lives by asking this question and being faithful to the answer. Since it is often very difficult to know exactly what Jesus would do in nuanced situations of the twenty-first century, a better question might be, "What *Did* Jesus Do?" Missionaries tempted by the greater good mentality might find "agency acceptable" alternatives to many steps that Jesus took, but these steps led Him to the cross to accomplish salvation for His people.

A study of Jesus' life reveals that He spent several years with His disciples teaching them, discipling them, and mentoring them, and then He sent them out. The need for speed and priming the pump for CPMs, where the ends often seem to justify the means, was not what Jesus did nor would do. Scratching the surface is sometimes argued to be better than never even touching the surface. Yet, we do not need to choose. The biblical approach is to do God's will where He leads us to do it, according to His gifting. If teaching, teach the people to observe all that the Lord commanded us. If the speed at which missionaries are moving will not allow such thorough and deep involvement, the truly greater good would be to slow down and watch God do what only He can do.

SUGGESTED READING

Dever, Mark. *Nine Marks of a Healthy Church.* Wheaton: Crossway, 2004.

_____. *What Is a Healthy Church?* Wheaton: Crossway, 2007.

Edwards, Jonathan. *The Surprising Work of God.* New Kensington, PA: Whitaker House, 1997.

Finney, Charles Grandison. *Lectures on Revivals of Religion.* New York: Leavitt, Lord & Co., 1835.

Hale, Thomas. *On Being a Missionary.* Pasadena, CA: William Carey Library, 2003.

Harris, J. Gerald. "Shining the Spotlight on the IMB's Church Planting Movement." *The Christian Index,* May 24, 2007.

Lewis, Tim and Rebecca Lewis. "Planting Churches: Learning the Hard Way." *Mission Frontiers* 31 (January/February 2009).

Meador, Clyde. "The Left Side of the Graph," *Journal of Evangelism and Missions* 6 (Spring 2007): 59–63.

Parshall, Phil. "Danger! New Directions in Contextualization." *Evangelical Missions Quarterly* 34:4 (October 1998): 404–10.

Winter, Ralph. "Two Responses," *Occasional Bulletin of the Evangelical Missiological Society* 22:1 (Winter 2009): 6–8.

8

EQUIPPING DISCIPLES: THEOLOGICAL EDUCATION AND THE MISSIONARY TASK

This chapter assumes the wisdom and cogent arguments made in the myriad books and articles that demonstrate the need for theological education and pastoral preparation, and it looks beyond them to understand why we must include theological education as an essential component of the task of international missions. We must remember all we have seen regarding the value of sound doctrine to combat the syncretism that insinuates itself into the churches in the absence of biblical truth. The purpose of theological education is to provide trained leadership for the churches and trained professors who can teach future church leaders, regardless of their location. Providing theological education in the many countries of the mission fields is vitally important. If it were not, the brightest and best could simply obtain student visas to come to the USA and study in any one of our theological seminaries or divinity schools. However, the education they would obtain would not adequately prepare national leaders for ministry in other contexts—even if they return to them, and sadly, they often do not.

TRAINING IN THE USA

There are two reasons against the practice of sending national pastors to the USA for training. The limited space of this chapter will not allow for either of them to be fully developed and explained, though they can be mentioned briefly.

First, when nationals from Global South countries with crippling economies, rampant diseases, underdeveloped infrastructures, unstable governments, warring neighbors, or little promise for the future come to the USA, it is common that the advantages they find here overwhelm their desire to return home. They may have come to the USA with altruistic intentions of returning and serving their people. However, while they are obtaining their education, their children grow up in the USA, and they begin to realize how very difficult it will be for their children to return to a land they never really knew. In the USA they have access to good public schools, medical care, police protection, and fully stocked grocery stores. Returning to the struggles of a Global South nation is often a daunting consideration. Generally, only the brightest and best students can obtain the visas and support to go abroad for study. When they succumb to the temptation to make a new life there and fail to return, the result is a "brain drain" that further cripples the churches in their homelands.

Second, even if the international student decides to return to his or her home country, their hard-won education may not be as applicable as they hoped. The content of the curriculum, teaching illustrations, and method of instruction often prepare the student for ministry in the USA much better than for ministry in an oral-based, agricultural country with a collectivistic, pre-modern worldview. We must include theological education as an essential part of the missionary task in the countries where we serve to address these concerns as well as others we will discuss later.

THE ROLE OF THEOLOGICAL EDUCATION

Theological education is not only essential for pastoral preparation, it provides a degree—and many national churches and their leaders desire this credentialing of graduates. One missionary to East Asia reported that the most common request he has received from the Chinese church leaders is for formal education that leads to credentials. This repeated request is heard the world over. Sometimes missionaries or administrators dismiss such a request, reasoning that it is a purely carnal desire that pales in comparison to the other needs that they must balance, even though the ones dismissing the request may hold advanced degrees themselves.

Theological education provides a cadre of pastors who have a respected seminary's seal of approval. Some churches around the world see the diplomas of a respected seminary as a sort of union card that they demand of their pastors. Many church members doubt their ability to recognize theological error when interviewing pastoral candidates. However, if the pastoral candidate has graduated from the respected seminary, they feel they can rest under his preaching and teaching, secure that he will teach the truth.

A basic and necessary function of a theological seminary or Bible college is to train pastors for the churches today as well as to equip the trainers of pastors for the churches of the future. Unfortunately, many who travel the world have witnessed the theological aberrations in churches and pastors where missionaries have relegated theological education to the realm of the unimportant or an optional luxury. Kevin Paszalek, lecturer at Kenya's Moffat Bible College, explained, "Even a well-intentioned person without some background in how to understand the Bible, how to interpret it, and how to apply it can get off track and take his whole church with him," yet even untrained men are valued. Paszalek continued, "One of the first pastors I ever met in Kenya walked a twenty-two mile circuit to pastor the three churches he was responsible for." The ministry of these committed servants is vital. One of the graduates, Pastor Charles Maina Macharia, remarked, "Sometimes the church dies without a pastor. Moffat training pastors is helping to produce pastors who will take care of the church of God."[1]

THE CHURCH OF THE POOR needs all the requisite skills to transmit the gospel faithfully as much as the church in the West does. It can make do without well-endowed seminaries, but it cannot do without sustained biblical learning and good theological educators.

—FONG CHOON SAM
Professor of Missions,
Baptist Theological Seminary, Singapore

The theological education and biblical preparation of pastors and leaders prepares them to recognize heretical developments that the church denounced long ago. Condemned heresies often continue to exist while morphing into different forms with new names, but educated Christians are able to see the error and avoid history repeating itself. Unfortunately, there are many examples where there is no training, and therefore heresy, doctrinal error, and syncretism have come to be so commonplace that they define the church in those areas.

HISTORICAL DANGERS AVOIDED

Just as merely having a military force does not guarantee that a country will never suffer a coup d'état or be attacked and overthrown, so theological education does not guarantee doctrinally sound theologians or heresy-proof churches. However, the country with no military virtually invites corruption and attack; and the church with no system for training pastors and leaders invites error and heresy.

If we were to list the television and radio preachers of today, how many on the list would we consider to be teaching some element of error? How much error is okay, and how much error must they be teaching to be dangerous—especially when they are teaching new believers? The infiltration of false prophets and teachers has always been a key strategy of the devil in his fight against God's people. The devil does not care if people have "mostly truth" if he can infect them with some error. In fact, he himself may give 99 percent of truth to lull them into complacency, as long as he can also inject his 1 percent of error. As in a rocket's trajectory, in the beginning we barely notice 1 percent of error, but after a few miles the rocket is badly off the plotted path to its intended destination. The church must be concerned for the truth because our Lord is truth. The devil cannot steal our salvation, thwart God's will, or prevail against Christ's church, but he constantly strategizes to inject error into the pure gospel and teachings of Christ.

As the gospel advances into previously untouched areas, the devil fights the hardest, knowing both that he is losing ground and that the new believers are at their most vulnerable stage of life. They are not yet sure of all they are to believe and are certainly not trained to recognize and refute error. Of all the places in the world, we should provide sound training and theological education on the mission fields, "Warning everyone and teaching everyone with all wisdom, that we may present everyone mature in Christ" (Colossians 1:28).

The devil has always warred against God's people with his "fifth column" in their midst. Nationalist General Emilio Mola coined the term *fifth column* during the Spanish Civil War of 1936–39. When he was leading his troops to attack Madrid, he was asked how he would conquer such a great city with four columns of soldiers. In a radio broadcast to encourage his troops and attack the morale of the Republican government, he said that his four columns would be joined by a fifth column that was already inside the city. The British people also employed this concept and term in the early years of World War II. They feared that the Germans living among them would strategically position themselves to help Hitler if he crossed the Channel to invade. The threat of the fifth column was the rationale for the mass internment of Germans on the Isle of Man during that war, just as the USA did with the Japanese who lived in America. The devil knows all about the fifth column strategy; he invented it. He seeks to confuse, divide, and conquer, and he uses false teachers to do so. Abandoning theological education is throwing open the gates of the city.

When false teachers come into the church, there is division in the body. We lose the unity that Christ told us to maintain, and when we lose that, we lose our witness and credibility (John 17:21). Therefore, when false teachers deceive and lead believers astray, man fails to achieve what God made him to do—to glorify God and to enjoy Him forever. In 2 Peter 2, Peter described the character and life of false teachers and the ethics that accompany false teachings. False prophets and teachers arose in the Old Testament and brought about syncretism, heresy, rebellion, and ultimately God's judgment. The New Testament also contains numerous admonitions to beware of false teachers, the leaven of the Pharisees, and the wolves in sheep's clothing. Paul warned the Ephesian elders that after his departure, "Fierce wolves will come in among you, not sparing the flock; and from among your own selves will arise men speaking twisted things, to draw away the disciples after them" (Acts 20:29–30).

In Paul's writings, he first teaches us what we are to believe and then how we are to live. What we think leads to what we do; what we believe leads to how we behave. Paul knew this foundational truth and thus concentrated in all of his letters on teaching theology first and then ethics. We can see this truth in the connection between a philosophy of missions and methodology; what you believe missions to be will affect how you go about it. It is for this reason that statements such as "Your ecclesiology will drive your missiology" are true. Theological education is vital for the health of the church in every country of the world. Without discipled shepherds holding sound theology, false teachers, prophets, and preachers may destroy the flock at will.

When the early church began to expand and Gentiles were coming to the Lord and into the church, there was an uproar over their inclusion. The controversy was so great that a council met to decide the issue and avert the crisis facing the young church. Having addressed what could have been a serious issue—either the danger of allowing Gentiles in without requiring them to become good Jews first, or the danger of allowing the controversy to rob the church of its unity and solid consensus—the council sent their decision to the churches of the world through the teaching of Paul and Barnabas. The result was both healing and blessing to the growth of the churches. "So the churches were strengthened in the faith, and they increased in numbers daily" (Acts 16:5). We would do well to consider how the story might have turned out if no one had been trained theologically to recognize the solution to the threat.

There have been many satanic attacks against the church through the centuries: the ante-Nicene heresies of Ebionism, Gnosticism, Montanism, or Manichaeism, and all of the trinitarian and Christological heresies of history. Ask yourself what kind of church we would have today if sound theologians had not confronted and overcome these errors. Imagine a version of church history where these threats were not only not taken seriously, there were no theologians trained well enough to address them if they had been—or worse, one where the church did not even know enough to recognize that they were dangerous theological aberrations!

Throughout history, the greatest theological minds periodically came together in councils to address threats to orthodox Christianity. History shows that these heresies never completely went away and are always popping back up. Indeed, the Bible teaches that there is nothing new under the sun (Ecclesiastes 1:9). For instance, the Jehovah's Witnesses cult, which teaches that Christ is a created being, is just another expression of the ancient Arian heresy that the Council of Nicea condemned in AD 325. When missionaries today give in to the need for speed and are enamored with missiological methodologies that are devoid of theological reflection, they fail to train the nationals to recognize and avoid the danger of these heresies.

Many cults are iterations of former errors. For instance, while there are many significant differences between Islam and the cult of Mormonism, there are also parallels of commonality that include aspects of their origins, male dominance, relocating the founding religious group, and allowing for multiple wives. Both religions grew out of one man's reinterpretation of the Old and New Testaments and retained much of them. They both believe the Bible to be a holy book, although inferior to their own. Significantly, in the origin of both, an angel appeared to guide the founders in the "correct" understanding of how to worship God. How necessary Paul's admonitions become in light of this aspect, "But even if we or an angel from heaven should preach to you a gospel contrary to the one we preached to you, let him be accursed" (Galatians 1:8). There is one gospel, once for all delivered to the saints, and the Bible warns us to be on our guard if even an angel should appear, claiming to be Gabriel, and gives us another gospel. God also taught His people, through Moses, to beware the constant threat of apostasy (Deuteronomy 13:1–3). Yet, how would we know that it is another gospel if no one has ever thoroughly grounded us in the true gospel?

Throughout church history theologians have come together to address such threats to the church. If those threats were real and dangerous then, they are real and dangerous when they appear today. In the absence of educated theologians and trained biblical scholars, fledgling churches will be at risk of repeating the past, but with a tragically different outcome.

It is for this reason that Paul wrote that ministers and churches should be very careful to believe, teach, and perpetuate sound doctrine (Romans 16:17; Ephesians 4:14; 1 Timothy 1:3, 10; 4:6; 6:3; Titus 1:9; 2:1, 10). In 1 Timothy 4:16, he wrote, "Keep a close watch on yourself and on the teaching. Persist in this, for by so doing you will save both yourself and your hearers." As a mentor, Paul modeled his exhortation to correct, rebuke, instruct, and exhort the churches. Paul taught that it matters what ministers and churches believe and teach because they must train others in right beliefs. Eckhard Schnabel wrote, "A further goal of Paul's missionary work was the training of new missionaries. The coworkers who accompanied Paul on his travels participated in his missionary activities and can thus be seen as trainees, much like Jesus' disciples who had been chosen by Jesus to be with him (Mark 3:13–15) and to be trained as 'fishers of people' (Mark 1:17)."[2] Throughout history, God has blessed theological education and pastoral preparation to enable His churches to recognize, confront, and avoid heresies that threatened them.

HISTORICAL DANGERS ESCAPED

Sadly, the pages of history are replete with instances of error creeping into the church. More often than not, this was because corrupt leaders were more adept in political maneuvering and more concerned with personal riches and power than they were with the Scriptures and bringing glory to God. During centuries of such abuse in, and of, the papal office, theological error was increasingly commonplace. Among other abuses, the Roman Catholic Church sold indulgences to raise money. These indulgences allowed the donors to erase years off of their pending purgatory time. Additionally, "celibate" priests and popes often had mistresses. In fact, some prostitutes of that era specialized in catering to a clientele of clergy members. The people were woefully ignorant of the Word of God because the Pope ruled that only the Roman Catholic Church could interpret the Bible. Unfortunately, those who could have interpreted the Word of God did not.

When the bride of Christ was languishing in such filth and corruption, God began to awaken men who would preach the truth and awaken the church. Martin Luther was one of the men whom God used. Luther had been a law student who became a monk after a life-threatening encounter during a thunderstorm. While practicing Roman Catholicism, Luther's legal mind sought peace with God. Reading the Bible and its warnings against sin caused Luther to suffer another thunderstorm, but this time it was the thundering of his conscience. He sought peace by every mechanism held forth in Roman Catholicism and found none. However, now a theologian and Bible scholar, he was searching the Scriptures and found therein the peace he had so long sought; "the righteous shall live by faith" (Romans 1:17). Theological error and lies were a saturating stench in the church of that time, but God used a theologian who studied the Word of God to open a window and allow the Spirit to blow through it. Luther was not alone in returning to the source of truth to find and preach the Truth; there were many others such as John Calvin and Ulrich Zwingli. Yet in every case, it was their understanding of the true teachings of the Word of God that caused them to recognize and rebel against error.

My YEARS AS A seminary student and teacher have put in me a love for those who live in the academic world. I can see how God has given them gifts to build up and enrich the body of Christ. Sometimes, these gifts appear esoteric to others, but they are no more or less valuable than other gifts God gives to members of His body. I continue to hope that the contribution of academics will be better recognized in the body of Christ in my country. The stewardship of our minds is an often-neglected ministry, and the body of Christ is weakened by its neglect.

—FONG CHOON SAM

Professor of Missions,
Baptist Theological Seminary, Singapore

Church history reveals that when denominations and churches abandon a high view of Scripture and sound theology, the death knell for orthodoxy often sounds among them. Seldom has a trek down heretical roads led any back to doctrinal health. One need only consider the prestigious Ivy League universities that started life as training institutions for pastors in Puritan New England and now serve as beacons of humanism and secularism.

However, in at least two situations, God has used sound theologians and biblical scholars who were firmly committed to His Word to bring about orthodox theological recovery. In the history of both the Southern Baptist Convention and The Southern Baptist Theological Seminary, God has shown that "those who honor me I will honor" (1 Samuel 2:30). In the convention of Southern Baptist churches, there was a time when theological liberalism weakened commitment to the truth of the Bible and orthodoxy. Professor Greg Wills ably argues the corresponding connection between theological liberalism in Southern Seminary and the resulting liberalism in the ranks of the churches: "The seminary began promoting the liberal religion around 1900. By the 1940s, the seminary's faculty consisted largely of liberals, and the school constituted the headwaters of most of the denomination's liberalism."[3] However, just as in Reformation history, God used theologians and biblical scholars to bring about a return to orthodoxy in the Southern Baptist Convention, as well as at Southern Seminary.

HISTORICAL DANGERS EMBRACED

Unfortunately, a lack of theological education has resulted in syncretism in many churches around the world. Those of us who have the privilege and opportunity of traveling to teach in many countries can trace a common thread as we go. I remember sharing a meal with some indigenous pastors in the Andes a few years ago and noticing that none of the pastors were drinking all of their drinks; they poured out the dregs of their glasses on the ground. I approached one of the senior pastors and pointed out to him that they seemed to be continuing the practice of giving the last of any food or drink to the earth goddess Pachamama. The pastor blushed when I mentioned I recognized what they were doing, but he defended it as a way to practice good ecology. I participated in a funeral for a toddler in an indigenous community and was surprised to see this evangelical family host a wake, funeral, and burial service that included mutually exclusive beliefs from Roman Catholicism, Andean animism, and the evangelical tradition.

Christian missionaries have worked in Africa for centuries. Yet in Nigeria, as discussed in chapter 1, the health and wealth gospel of evangelical-type churches blends seamlessly with ancestor veneration and juju magic of traditional animism. Pastors complain that their members might be in church in the morning and in the witch doctor's hut in the afternoon. The AIC churches are wildly diverse churches that claim to be Christian but include magic, reincarnations of Jesus—or any of the prophets—and heretical beliefs. Each of them has some connection with the truth in the past, but the dearth of sound instruction has allowed divergent religious heresies to develop.

As mentioned earlier, if anyone could point to a success story in the African church, it would have been in Rwanda, the most "Christian" country in Africa . . . until one tribe turned on another and almost a million people were murdered. Yes, there were many Christians among them, and they had the Bible, but the Christianity was merely nominal. Culturally appropriate theological education with biblical application of the Scriptures was absent. Rwanda Institute of Evangelical Theology graduate Alexis Nemeyimana reported, "We used the Bible in church, but we didn't really *think biblically*, or always *teach the Bible accurately*" (emphasis added).[4] The mind-numbing numbers of people massacred, as well as those who were swinging the machetes to kill them during the bloodshed, point to the painful absence of biblical evangelical Christianity.

In many ways, animism continues as strongly as it did before Christianity came among evangelicals in the Mexican countryside. Combining Christianity with former animistic religions has resulted in many manifestations of confused syncretism. For instance, in one region, men who kill an animal for a traditional barbecue place the knives used to butcher it in the cooking fire in the shape of the cross, believing that this will protect those who eat the meat from the spirit of the animal. When women feed a log into a cooking fire, they always place the fatter end of the log in first, believing that this will enable their babies to come out headfirst in the birth process. In the absence of sound theological teaching and biblical instruction, traditions develop from syncretism and become as authoritative as

Scripture. Believers often live out what they have learned, but the teaching they have received has not been contextualized and has not conveyed the Bible's teachings to their culture. One missionary to China said that the believers there know how to evangelize but they do not know much else; no one has taught them.

THEOLOGICAL EDUCATION AROUND THE WORLD

The current state of theological education around the world varies from country to country. Countless people groups have the need for theological training but no existing programs. Eustace Karangwa, president of the Evangelical Alliance of Rwanda, said, "Most of the churches are really in a great need of trained pastors, but have no people who are trained to come help us."[5] In many countries, theological education is sadly lacking, if it exists at all, because the missionaries have abandoned theological education to conduct evangelism and church planting. Even if that was not the case, missionaries often did not leave a theologically sound institution behind since their own education did not ground them firmly in the Word. Often, missionaries trained in seminaries influenced by the liberal trends in the USA sow that theology on the mission field. Additionally, Global South economies frequently do not allow their own churches to support the seminaries as the Western missionaries did when they established them. Seminaries left in the care of the national churches lack operating funds as well as basic books and supplies.

Current Models

Many mission agencies still report profound involvement in theological education around the world. Some agencies advertise open positions in theological education to maintain good public relations with their constituency or to attract more applicants, but interested candidates would be wise to look under the hood and kick the tires; all that glitters is not gold. Much of what is reported as theological education is neither theological nor education.

Sometimes missionaries conduct one-day workshops to instruct pastors how to form a new church, hold witnessing seminars, or even conduct stewardship classes to teach tithing. All of these are needed, but many missionaries count them as theological education. When the agency tallies the number of participants and reports them as theology students, the numbers may be quite impressive, but not honest. Another example is the Training for Trainers model, also known as T4T. This program aims to train people to start house churches, not to educate them theologically or biblically. "Just-in-time" training is another model that many count as theological education. With this model, the teacher gives needed information to the church planter the day he needs it. One missionary described it as a mother duck with all her ducklings walking behind. All the duckling needs to know is where to step next. As long as it is following closely and watching, it will receive the needed instruction in time. Another missionary who had found this method lacking reported in frustration that when just-in-time training is used for training new believers in theology and Bible knowledge, it is most often not just-in-time, but also too little, too late.

Theological Education by Extension

Beginning in the 1960s, missionaries in Guatemala began to experiment with a decentralized education model. They called their new model Theological Education by Extension (TEE). Missionaries such as Ralph D. Winter and Ross Kinsler recognized that they were not training enough leaders for the churches. Furthermore, they noticed that they were not always training the right ones among those who were being trained. The men who were pastoring the churches were those who were literally elders; they had families and farms and could not go to the capital cities where the seminaries were located. The ones who could do so were young men who may not develop in maturity with the gifts and character that God's Word requires. Moreover, missionaries also learned that the churches would not accept a young man as pastor. Therefore, they wisely took the seminary to the students, sending professors to the churches to conduct classes instead of the students coming to them. Merkle believes that this model is more in harmony with what Paul did. He wrote,

> We would be mistaken, however, if we suppose that theological education on the mission field must be carried out precisely how it is in the West. As a missionary, Paul would visit various churches seeking to establish them in the gospel. Those who received training and instruction did not go to Paul. On the contrary, Paul went to them and trained them in their local setting where they could continue to work, raise their families, and lead the church. . . . In some circumstances, and perhaps in most circumstances among newly reached people groups, formal theological education should not be the preferred method of training. The crucial factor is that some on-going training takes place to ensure the viability of the Christian faith.[6]

Other models of decentralized theological education today are correspondence course programs in which students study and send in completed lessons, or they listen to lessons and receive pastoral training over the radio as with HCJB Global's radio broadcast Bible Institute of the Air.

In predominantly preliterate areas, seminary programs consist of completely oral instruction. This is not only necessary due to their preliteracy; it is in step with the wisdom of training in culturally appropriate ways. "Current estimates indicate that around two-thirds of the world's population are oral communicators either by necessity or by choice. To effectively communicate with them, we must defer to their oral communication style. Our presentations must match their oral learning styles and preferences. Instead of using outlines, lists, steps, and principles we need to use culturally relevant approaches they would understand."[7] Insisting on the necessity of theological education around the world does not naively presume that everyone learns the same way but reminds us that our responsibility is to train believers to interpret and apply the Bible in ways that are faithful to sound theology *and* sensitive to the culture.

A cursory review of existing seminary programs reveals that the most effective programs in traditional mission fields are also those that incorporate a strong practicum in the curriculum. Some require students to plant a church before they can graduate. Others include mission trips and regular witnessing as part of the core requirements. Theological education does not have to be formal; it may be very informal. Lifelong continuing education can include lay training courses, retreats, conferences, or even mentoring relationships. The form does not matter as long as it is culturally appropriate and that we remember the most important component is training them to interpret and apply God's Word faithfully and effectively.

THE NEED TO RETURN TO THEOLOGICAL EDUCATION

The greatest need of the burgeoning worldwide church is for more theologically trained pastors and teachers. Heresies and aberrant forms of Christianity abound in the absence of sound seminaries to train church leaders. Many institutions have lost personnel and financial resources with little warning, and they are having trouble carrying on the work. I have taught and ministered in struggling evangelical seminaries in many countries of North America, Central America, the Caribbean, South America, Europe, Africa, and Asia. I have encountered empty bookstore shelves, dusty libraries where worms caused great destruction to the books, too many students with too few professors, and many students confused about matters of doctrine. Many countries have countless church members who are merely Christians in name or ethnicity. Bruce Rossington, Acting Principal of the Rwanda Institute of Evangelical Theology, said of the state of the church during the genocide, "What happened in 1994 has thrown everything into question. Nominal Christianity has been seen to be useless. It's no good. It didn't stop what was going on. I believe there is a real thirst for true spiritual meaning. People are looking for answers to big questions."[8] John Stam wrote of the doctrinal chaos that exists in Latin America, "Big sectors of the Latin American church, even more than in the US, seem to stagger from one shallow, sensational fad to another. For a while, it was 'name it, claim it' or 'holy laughter and spiritual warfare.' Then there was 'health and wealth,' which has morphed into the even more lopsided 'theology of prosperity.' . . . Knocking people to the floor has become very popular, as has the latest novelty of naming 'apostles.'"[9]

These are simply symptoms of a greater disease; the churches have largely departed from the use of the Bible as its only rule of faith and practice. No one meant for this to happen, but as we've seen, new strategies for reaching the world as quickly as possible often included abandoning theological education. Many times, theological liberals stepped into teaching positions when sound agencies pulled out. It is time to return and give renewed emphasis to theological education in the missionary task, because the churches are filling the vacuum of empty seminary classrooms with syncretism and heresy.

OPPORTUNITIES IN THEOLOGICAL EDUCATION

The opportunities and invitations to return to the classrooms are coming not only from the churches; the struggling seminaries are also begging for help. Governments and accrediting agencies often demand more than the nationals can provide, which effectively closes many evangelical seminaries. David Bledsoe wrote of Brazil, "Opportunities exist to return to the historic mission fields to help reestablish Christian theology and reinforce a mission emphasis among some established evangelical denominations."[10] Randy Smith, founder and president of Youth Ministry International, has initiated a program that sends professors to train trainers who can train future leaders for youth ministry. This has been particularly effective in places like Cuba, where missionaries cannot serve as resident missionaries.

FOR THREE YEARS I directed an intensive, semester-long discipleship program for enthusiastic, college-age men and women. Only about a dozen students were admitted each term in order to foster an environment where authentic relationships could flourish amid rigorous theological training and spiritual disciplines. Together we explored God's Word, prayed, studied, worshiped, underwent physical challenges, and served our community —all an embodied response to the Holy Spirit's work in us to "will and to act according to his good purpose" (Philippians 2:13 NIV). I believe that this sort of intensive and intimate training of Christian leaders is essential to the task of missions in our age.

—DAVID SONJU
Former director of the LIFT Discipleship Program

SOLUTIONS: A WAY FORWARD

The most important corrective is for missionaries to follow God's call on their lives. God knows His churches' needs, and He has heard their cry. He is calling, gifting, and guiding many to career service as theological educators just as He called Moses to lead Israel from their bondage. Formal theological education with Master of Divinity and doctoral degrees through classic classroom instruction are not necessarily the answer. There are numerous models for theological education, leadership training, and pastoral preparation. Some are adaptations of generations-old training models found in the cultures of the world such as "watch-and-do" learning, the master-apprentice model, and on-the-job training. Missionaries should avoid the trap of thinking that they must train the nationals in the same way in which they received training. An understanding of the content is more important than the style of teaching used to convey it.

The greatest model of sound doctrine, effective teaching, and clear biblical application can be found in the pastoral ministries of the Puritans. Many of them had no formal theological training. They may have had training in the classics and several languages, but they learned the depths of their theology and scriptural application on their knees and in mentoring relationships. After quoting a passage from the Puritan Baptist John Bunyan's *Pilgrim's Progress* where Bunyan described the life and work of the Interpreter, Sinclair Ferguson stated that this also described the Puritan minister. Ferguson wrote, "All the ingredients of the Puritan view of ministry can be seen in this single portrait: the basic qualification of personal godliness and giftedness coupled with single-minded learning in the interpretation of the Scripture; a spirit of prayerfulness; a deep care for the people of God; and the ability to unfold the mysteries of the gospel in a manner which reached into men's hearts and touched their consciences—and all set within the context of a prayerful dependence on the Lord."[11] For Ferguson, this was the essence of a godly pastor. He went on to describe the Puritan minister: ". . . the Puritans sought to marry *learning* to their spirituality."[12]

How did such great learning and ministerial character come about? Ferguson described weekly gatherings of the Puritan ministers for conversation where the younger ones learned from the older ones. After describing how they learned their theology in this way, he wrote, "It would be mistaken, however, to think that in lacking a seminary, theological college, or divinity faculty education these men lacked a biblical and theological education itself. Their learning in areas of biblical study and theology would have left most of them unembarrassed in the company of a modern graduate in theology."[13] The training of nationals need not mirror the high literacy of academia with all the trappings of the Western tradition. However, it must train the disciples, who will be the future church leaders, in culturally appropriate ways. One such method was mentoring, found in both the Puritan model and in countless cultures today, to understand God's Word within a theologically sound framework and be able to communicate that truth to others. The thousands of cultural contexts of the world dictate that theological education will not always look the same, but the substance of biblical instruction and application should always be the same and must always be present.

CONCLUSION

The status quo of theologically shallow churches and poorly equipped pastors cannot continue; too much is at risk. Many mission agencies are connected with theologically sound USA-based seminaries that are in a perfect position to forge partnerships to train brothers and sisters in the Southern Church. David Bledsoe points out that the goal of partnerships is not to reestablish the mission's control—or even permanent presence—in the historical mission fields, but rather to use the focus on theological education as a means by which church planting and church growth is expanded.[14]

Not only do the most effective seminary models not slow down the work of evangelism and church planting, they enhance it. National churches, mission agencies, missionaries, and theological seminaries must work together to stop the brain drain that often occurs when students go abroad for education and do not return. They can begin to plug the drain by training the right people the right way—in the cultural context and by not exporting them to other countries or capital cities for their education. The right people are the ones who will be accepted as pastors and leaders. The right content means more than a mere translation of what the Western missionary-professor learned in seminary. The theological issues pertinent to the culture, such as the dominant religion—whether Islam, Roman Catholicism, Hinduism, or Buddhism—need greater attention than the Western-context seminary gave it. Certainly, as with Bunyan's Interpreter, the minister is more than a theologically equipped brain; ministry skills, godly character, leadership, and administrative skills are all necessary. Many of these aspects cannot be taught; they are better caught. Therefore, mentors are needed to model what God wants to see in us.

It is time for missionaries and missiologists to slow down their breakneck pace of ever-increasing speeds and return to fulfilling the Great Commission to make disciples by teaching them to observe all that Jesus commanded us. There exists a worldwide need to make sound theology the priority among the churches—especially those where strategies seek to attain a population of 2 percent evangelicals and leave. We must find the balance between strategies to "preach Christ where He has never been named" and "presenting everyone perfect in Christ Jesus."

Suggested Reading

Burton, Sam Westman. *Disciple Mentoring: Theological Education by Extension.* Pasadena, CA: William Carey Library, 1998.

Claydon, David, ed. "A New Vision, A New Heart, A Renewed Call." In *Lausanne Occasional Papers from the 2004 Forum for World Evangelization.* Pasadena, CA: William Carey Library, 2006.

Dever, Mark and Sinclair Ferguson. *The Westminster Directory of Public Worship.* Hagerstown, MD: Christian Heritage, 2008.

Elliston, Edgar J., ed. *Teaching Them Obedience in All Things: Equipping for the 21st Century.* Pasadena, CA: William Carey, 1999.

Kinsler, F. Ross, ed. *Diversified Theological Education.* Pasadena, CA: William Carey, 2007.

Kinsler, F. Ross. *The Extension Movement in Theological Education: A Call to the Renewal of the Ministry.* Pasadena, CA: William Carey Library, 1978.

Kirwen, Michael C., ed. *A Model Four Semester Syllabus for Transcultural Theology Overseas.* Lewiston, NY: The Edwin Mellen Press, 1986.

Stackhouse, Max L. *Apologia: Contextualization, Globalization, and Mission in Theological Education.* Grand Rapids: Eerdmans Publishing, 1988.

Winter, Ralph D., ed. *Theological Education by Extension.* Pasadena, CA: William Carey Library, 1969.

9

PRIMARY ORAL LEARNERS: HOW SHALL THEY HEAR?

Over 70 percent of the world's population consists of people who are oral learners—people who cannot or will not read. An even greater percentage of the people being targeted as unreached people groups are preliterate, primary oral learners who cannot read or write the language that they speak—often because their language has not yet been reduced to writing. Their lives are lived out in an oral fashion. They learn about events in their world, form their opinions, share knowledge, and entertain one another using only the spoken word.[1] Their preliteracy precludes the use of traditional educational models that utilize classrooms, note-taking, reading, and research. Many missionaries have concluded that primary oral learners pose too great a problem for those desiring to train them. However, others have found great success using education methods that require no literacy whatsoever. Oral education models employ memorization, storytelling, songs, proverbs, drama, and chanting. Today's challenge of training primary oral learners is not new.

HISTORICAL CONSIDERATIONS

Missionaries have historically found little success when utilizing traditional Western church, discipleship, and training methodologies among oral cultures. Missiologists have also learned that literates do not naturally interact effectively with oral cultures. Even when missionaries dedicate the time and effort to learn the languages of their target mission fields, clear communication is often difficult. Moreover, oral cultures do not understand, learn, remember, retell, or process new information in the same way that literate cultures do. This frustration causes many missions agencies to wither before the challenge of educating primary oral learners and prefer simply to evangelize them and leave them to grow spiritually on their own. Yet, the preliteracy of primary oral learners is not too great a barrier to training; the key is to communicate with them in culturally appropriate ways.

An outpouring of the Holy Spirit among the Highland Quichua people of the Andes in the 1960s and 1970s resulted in many pockets of evangelicals among them. Some skeptics questioned the nature of this people movement, especially when its growth rate began to plateau in the 1980s. Since I was ministering among this people group and working on my first doctoral degree, I chose to analyze and evaluate the movement to determine whether it was spurious or genuine. The research concluded that the movement was indeed genuine, but also revealed that there were very few pastors among them and virtually no way for pastors to be trained appropriately.

The Holy Spirit had called out a number of men as pastors and leaders, but the only pastoral training programs were in the large cities and conducted in Spanish. Additionally, these Western-style seminaries required the preliterate, oral culture Quichua student to be highly literate. The student also needed to have job skills to support himself in a modern city. Quichua men who were serving as pastors could not leave their subsistence farms, families, and churches for training in the city, even if they could learn Spanish and literacy skills. Therefore, some sincere missionaries chose a few teenage boys who were ambitious and eager to serve. They brought the young men into their homes in the cities, provided their needs, and taught them Spanish and literacy in order to be educated in seminary. Unfortunately, those who received this training were not accepted as elders and leaders in the traditional Quichua communities since they were seen as mere boys. Thus, even the few that had been trained were not accepted as pastors or valued as spiritual leaders.

IF I COULD SUM UP my eight years of missionary service in the French Overseas Departments, it would be this. I worked tirelessly at worldview profiling and ethnographic interviewing. When I arrived at a clear and basic understanding of the people I was trying to reach, I developed Bible-based discipleship curriculum that was staged and incremental. I put it in pamphlets and books. It was quality work. There was only one problem. The people were oral.

By the time I left the field, I was discovering how to do oral catechisms. This was not typical for a Baptist. I wish I could turn back the clock and do spoken, stepped teaching and learning from the very beginning. My disciples would have been far more grounded and able to reproduce in an oral environment.

—DAN SHEARD
Senior Pastor, Calvary Missionary Baptist Church
Adjunct Instructor, Lincoln University

This challenge led me to conduct research in a second dissertation on the subject: "Highland Quichuas: Discovering a culturally appropriate pastoral training model." This grew out of my burden for the Quichua people and passion to discover ways to train leaders among them. Primary oral learners like the Highland Quichuas make up the majority of the peoples in the traditional mission fields and rapidly growing segments of the people groups in the Western world as well. They also represent one of the greatest challenges facing missionaries today. Therefore, we would be wise to learn more about them, how they think, how they process new information, and how we can reach and teach them.

WORLDVIEW AND CULTURE

The worldview of the primary oral learner must be understood if its people are to be effectively engaged with the gospel. The International Orality Network defines an oral learner as "1. Someone who cannot read or write. 2. Someone whose most effective communication and learning format, style, or method is in accordance with oral formats, as contrasted to literate formats. 3. Someone who prefers to learn or process information by oral rather than written means. (These are literate people whose preferred communication style is oral rather than literate, even though they can read.)"[2]

Primary oral learners do not process information in the same manner that highly literate learners in the Western world have been trained to do. From kindergarten forward, highly literate societies progressively teach children to reason, to use syllogisms in logic for problem solving, and to think conceptually using abstract ideas. These are learned abilities that are not shared innately by primary oral learners. The relatively new field of ethnocognition studies the ways in which people groups think and reason. It is new because such a basic level of engaging daily life, understanding the world around us, and processing cause and effect relationships seems to be just plain common sense, and we marvel that someone would do so differently. In fact, we question the intelligence of someone who does not view life as we do. We overlook the fact that the reasoning skills we possess, our linear, sequential logic, and the syllogisms we employ for making sense of reality are learned, not innate. They are woven into the fabric of the most basic levels of our culture and worldview. However, primary oral learners have not been to the schools we attended, and most often, they have not been to a school at all. They learned what they know through their own personal experience or through the life skills and wisdom of people they know and trust. Instructing them using bullet points, steps in a plan, outlines, or detailed instructions is ineffective. Oral cultures are face-to-face cultures and prefer a watch-and-do method of education.

Worldview and reality are intricately woven together in the minds of people. A person's worldview is what answers the important questions of life. "What is real?" "Where do people come from?" "Where do they go when they die?" "Where does sickness come from?" A culture's worldview enables its members to make sense of their world. It is literally how they view the world. Missiologist Charles Kraft defines it this way, "These worldview assumptions, values, and commitments may be likened to a window through which human beings look out on reality. . . . Our worldview, like every other aspect of our culture, is taught to us from birth, and so convincingly that most of us never question that our view of reality is the only accurate one. Our deep-level worldview perspectives provide us with our understandings of both the personal and the nonpersonal universes around us."[3] The late missionary-anthropologist and missions professor Paul G. Hiebert wrote, "Taken together, the basic assumptions about reality which lie behind the beliefs and behavior of a culture are sometimes called a world view."[4]

Worldview is a subset of culture[5], which in turn could be said to be a subset of worldview. Since culture is learned and shared in a society as it is developed in and passed on from one generation to the next, the worldview of those shaping cultural norms, values, behavior, rituals, and other aspects of daily life is influencing every component. In turn, this entire process incrementally informs one's view of reality, or worldview. The symbiotic relationship between worldview and culture defines reality for any people group.

Worldview—along with culture—is imparted to children from parents, grandparents, pastors, teachers, siblings, friends, advertising, music lyrics, proverbs, chants, legends, movies, pop culture, and other influencers. The stories of our lives and societies give order and meaning to mundane events and tragedies alike. When a missionary shares a story from a radically different worldview without taking the target culture's worldview into account, the message is nonsense to the hearer. The missionary's well-intentioned meaning is muddled or lost altogether.

In the well-known missions video *EE-taow!*, Mark Zook engages a tribe of people who believe that they came from the union of two jungle birds. This was the accepted origin myth among them. The problem was that Mark needed to tell them biblical truth about the creation of the world and it would make no sense to them that some deity had made the world *ex nihilo* while they were trying to understand it within the worldview of the jungle-bird-origin myth. Therefore, he began to chip away at their worldview with casual inquiries into the details of their long-held beliefs. He asked one elder whether anyone had ever witnessed a jungle bird bringing forth humans. Mark also questioned the cultural "flood-maker" as to whether he could flood the forest even when it did not rain. Stumping the Mouk elders with hard questions created uncomfortable gaps in their worldview. When they began to question the veracity of their old stories, they were increasingly ready to hear new ones. Mark then told the story of the Bible to give them a biblical worldview in which they could understand biblical truth and their need for a Savior. The new stories radically changed their worldview.

Bridges and Barriers

In every people group, there will be barriers to accepting the gospel message. These barriers can be things such as traditional religions, sin, or fear of losing riches. There will also be gaps that existing worldviews cannot explain—especially as the Western world encroaches and brings with it modern marvels. Yet God has not left Himself without witness in the cultures of the world. By His grace and providence, there will also be bridges over which missionaries can take the gospel message.

Don Richardson wrote of his experience of finding such a bridge in *Peace Child*. He settled among the Sawi in Papua New Guinea, a cannibalistic tribe that was constantly warring with neighboring tribes. After he had learned their language and told them the message of the gospel, the men began to celebrate Judas as the hero of the story. They explained to a confused Richardson that in their culture it was a high virtue to win someone's friendship, and when he least expects it, to kill and eat him. Treachery was the highest virtue. Due to this barrier to the gospel, Richardson despaired of ever seeing Christianity established among such ruthless people.

When they learned of his plans to leave them, they promised not to war with the neighboring tribe if he would only stay, since he was the source of medicines and conveniences from the outside world. He doubted their sincerity and asked them how they would make peace, since the enemy tribe would surely suspect treacherous intentions. They explained to him that they had a ritual among them that would result in peace with their enemies. In the ritual, the chief of Richardson's tribe gave his son to the chief of the neighboring tribe. The child was referred to as the peace child. It was explained that as long as the boy continued in good health, there would be peace between them. This gave Richardson the bridge that God had left for reaching this Stone Age tribe.

He retold the gospel story, but this time he referred to Jesus as the peace child, telling the story in a way that the culture could understand. When he got to Judas' betrayal of Jesus, the tribesmen were despondent. He tried to tell them that this was the same story that he told before, but they did not agree. They said that he had not told them that Jesus was the peace child before and that the worst thing that anyone could do would be to hurt the peace child. In this way God showed Richardson that within this culture there was a redemptive analogy that He had provided for sharing the truth of the gospel.

The traditional cultures of the world present unique challenges, but God always provides a way. In the situation above, many missionaries would be thrilled to see that the Sawi people had accepted Christ upon hearing the gospel, and they would consider their work done. The Sawi had no written language, no understanding of any other major language that had the Bible, no libraries filled with reference tools, and no educational system for teaching pastors. Some would say that they ought to be able to find their way; after all, they had the Holy Spirit to lead them into all truth. It is at this point that many missionaries would choose to move on to evangelize the next group. However, the challenges of teaching primary oral learners "to observe all that I have commanded you" do not allow missionaries to follow the path of least resistance.

LITERACY AND GOD'S WORD

As I have described, one of the challenges missionaries face is the low, or nonexistent, literacy level of many peoples in the world. The way most of us came to know the Lord, were discipled, and perhaps even called into missions, was through reading and reflecting upon God's Word. In the foreword to Herbert Klem's book *Oral Communication of the Scripture*, Charles Kraft says, "Indeed, we have become so locked into the assumption that people come to and grow in Christ largely through reading the Bible that we can hardly imagine how (or that) God could have worked before Gutenberg!"[6]

However, when Jesus walked along the shore of the Sea of Galilee and taught the people of His day, He did not use a highly literate education model. Less than 10 percent of the people of His day were literate, so He used a method of teaching that incorporated illustrations, stories, and parables. He would say, "The kingdom of heaven is like . . ." and then give them a real-world illustration that they could visualize. The world of preliteracy is difficult for Christians today to imagine. However, it was not until 1455 that Johann Gutenberg invented the printing press with movable type; it was an invention that revolutionized the world much like the Internet has done in our own time. Prior to Gutenberg's printing press, only the educated elite could read. The printed word was not widely available, and it would take up to two years for a team of monks to copy the Bible. After Gutenberg, Bibles, liturgies, theological treatises, and sermons were being printed, and Christians were learning to read. Wherever Christians went they established churches, and next door to the church, they started a school. In some areas of the world reading was so essential in Christian thinking that literacy became a requirement to join the church and be baptized. Christianity and literacy became virtually synonymous in much of Christianity's thinking. It has been noted that since Gutenberg, Christianity has walked on literate feet.[7]

WITHOUT PASTORAL TRAINING and theological education for oral learners, it would be hard for a leader to care for a church. The challenge is for the missionary-trainer to contextualize teaching, but to assume and encourage a literacy improvement among the national leaders. One of the greatest social ministries we can offer on the mission field today is literacy training and not assume that leaders will want to continue to be oral learners. The Bible was written down, and I think we must remember that the Lord, in His wisdom, had it written, thus showing a benefit in moving the redeemed and their ecclesiastical leaders toward literacy.

—DAVID BLEDSOE

*Urban evangelist and church planting trainer,
Brazil*

Missionaries assume that preliterate nationals want to learn to read and are shocked when they discover that in many instances no such desire exists. Missionaries typically come from cultures where illiteracy is viewed with a jaundiced eye and is a negative, pejorative trait associated with the dregs of society—something from which people need to be rescued. Yet, in many countries, literacy rates are still at the same levels that Jesus encountered in His ministry.

Most governments are eager to develop their infrastructures and economies. They compete for multinational corporations to come and build factories and invest in their countries. Yet, they realize that a literate workforce is desired for companies to consider this as a possibility. The desire to enhance their country's image and attract outside help often leads to an exaggeration of the actual literacy level.

Oftentimes, governments look to banking or voting statistics as a way to measure literacy, since signing one's name is required for both, and some use that ability as a test for literacy. When we left Ecuador to return to the USA, we asked our friend and helper to give us her address so we could write and stay in touch. She said, "Oh, I am so sorry, I cannot read or write; I only know how to sign my name." We had seen her carefully sign her name on numerous occasions and so were shocked to learn that she was preliterate. We were also saddened by this, not only because we would not be able to stay in touch, but because we would have gladly spent time teaching her to read and write had we known. Signing one's name is not proof of literacy. Other governments consider someone who has graduated from the fourth grade to be literate. However, someone may have graduated from the fourth grade forty years ago and not have read a word since. He would hardly be literate. Such people may be able to write their own name, or even read the headlines in a newspaper, but they do not function in the literate world.

Embarrassment often causes preliterates to hide their limitations from literate Westerners. People may claim to be able to read so others will not look down on them. Others will not attempt literacy classes, as they fear failure. In other instances the children may be learning to read and write in school and the older members of the family employ a self-defense mechanism of relegating literacy to the level of children's games. When this happens, even the children begin to view reading in the same light and long for the day when they grow up and can set it aside. Herbert Klem reports that literacy ministries in Africa found that even after attaining reading and writing skills, many communities returned to living as an oral culture. Some missionaries believe that teaching literacy skills is the simple key for bringing oral cultures into the twenty-first century. Klem writes, "However, after nearly one hundred years of mission and government literacy training programs, the number of people who can or will read to gain vital information is very small. In some areas literacy approaches 25 percent, but in most rural areas it is likely to be less than 5 percent."[8]

ORALITY, EVANGELISM, AND DISCIPLESHIP

The number of people who are considered highly literate make up only 20–30 percent of the world's population.[9] These are people who can pick up an unfamiliar book, read it, comprehend its message, reflect upon it, and write a reasoned response. Just imagine that the people who do not have this ability make up 70–80 percent of the world's population. However, throughout the history of Christianity, the majority of evangelical churches have been in the minority of the world that is highly literate. We have not concentrated efforts on how to reach and teach the nations as they are.

Highly literate people communicate using lists, tables, outlines, diagrams, graphs, steps, and abstract concepts. Primary oral learners communicate using stories, repetition, proverbs, traditional sayings, legends, songs, chanting, poetry, and drama. Sadly, less than 10 percent of ministry tools, evangelism programs, and discipleship resources are designed to meet the needs of the preliterate oral cultures.[10] Those who are counted among the unreached people groups as well as millions of people among "reached" groups are predominantly preliterate, oral culture peoples. How then can we reach and teach them?

Chronological Bible Storying (CBS) is one effective tool for evangelizing, discipling, and training oral culture peoples. Using this tool, missionaries can give the Bible to people in an oral format in the same chronological order that God has given it in the written Word. Rather than preaching sermons on selected verses without the context of the whole counsel of the Word of God, CBS seeks to give hearers the Bible in a culturally appropriate manner and develop a biblical worldview regarding God, creation, sin, sacrifice, and salvation. The missionary tells the stories to communicate basic Bible truths that the hearers need to know for the gospel to make sense. Additionally, by missionaries' telling the Bible message using stories told in culturally appropriate ways, the hearers will be able to understand, remember, and retell the stories to others. One of the primary concepts of Chronological Bible Storying is that people cannot understand the gospel message when trying to "hear" it in an unbiblical worldview.

I FIND MYSELF spending hours weekly sitting under trees with Africans discussing the Scripture using oral Bible stories. We listen, we take time—even several weeks on one story—to think and discuss about how to accurately and meaningfully re-express the story in their heart language. I believe this process is one way to fulfill the "teaching them to obey everything" that is time consuming to execute but ultimately the heart of the Great Commission. I have seen misunderstandings slowly unraveled, the truth clearly expressed, and transformations celebrated. This kind of ministry is harder to quantify and the numbers do not seem impressive. However, syncretism cannot be understood, confronted, and eliminated in an afternoon. Discipling is the slow process of mentoring Africans in how to handle Scripture so it can transform their lives and culture and give them a process which they can use to disciple others.

—STAN WAFLER
Missionary, Northwest Uganda

The Word of God is filled with stories. Many of us heard Old and New Testament stories from our mothers, in Sunday school, and in Vacation Bible School throughout childhood. These stories have shaped our understanding of God and life. When Jesus wanted to teach His oral learners, He did not choose an Old Testament text and preach a three-point sermon, although He certainly could have done so; He told stories. For instance, in Luke 15, Jesus told three stories to make one point to His hearers. He talked about a lost sheep, a lost coin, and a lost son. Each of the stories had the same main point: the thing that was lost was precious to the one who lost it and there was great rejoicing when it was found. Any of His hearers could have gone home and repeated these stories and their main point to their family.

Some wonder about the value of CBS for communicating Bible truths when they consider the portion of the Bible that is didactic instead of narrative. For instance, how would one tell the story of the book of James, or Romans, or the Sermon on the Mount? Daniel Sheard explains how to teach these portions to oral learners in *An Orality Primer for Missionaries*. He demonstrates that repeating short questions and answers throughout the lesson is very effective for teaching such passages. Utilizing short pithy phrases, questions and answers, and frequent repetition when teaching oral cultures is not a new method.

In Tom Nettles's collection of Baptist catechisms, he includes E. T. Winkler's 1857 *Notes and Questions for the Oral Instruction of Colored People*.[11] Winkler's catechism was found to be a useful tool for teaching preliterate peoples. When we were serving in Ecuador, this inspired us to use a simple catechism for the oral instruction of Highland Quichua believers in the Andes. Participants grew in their knowledge of Christian doctrine and enjoyed the friendly competition of knowing the right answers.

Any oral instructional method utilized should also include a time of thorough examination to determine whether the lessons have been properly learned. This examination, or discovery session, may consist of asking the learners to repeat the story. Repeating the story not only solidifies the story in the minds of everyone, but also allows the teacher to identify inaccuracies that would otherwise be perpetuated. In addition to a time of repetition, the storyer should include a question period to determine comprehension of the story. In this way, the teacher may identify problem areas of his storytelling or inadequacies of his language skills in the target culture. Asking the hearers how the lesson should be applied to their lives will also ensure that they have grasped the point of the lesson and will be able to teach it to others accurately. This also provides an opportunity to correct any incorrect application that could have been made from the lesson before it finds its way into the community. Again, the primary point of using culturally appropriate teaching techniques for primary oral learners is so they can understand, remember, and repeat the stories to others and remain faithful to the truth.

Telling the Bible stories chronologically allows the hearer to develop a biblical worldview of who God is, what God thinks about sin, what sacrifice is, and why God sent His Son to die on the cross. Indeed, hearing the Bible stories from creation to the cross will leave the hearer breathless with anticipation as the stories of the birth and life of Jesus are told. The crucifixion and resurrection stories will have a totally different impact upon those who have developed a biblical worldview from hearing Bible stories than a simple sermon on John 3:16 will have upon animistic tribal people who have never heard of God, sin, Jesus, heaven, or hell.

Missionaries should spend time learning the worldview of their target culture so as to identify the bridges and barriers to the gospel. Certainly, no one could "tell" every single page of the Bible to their target oral culture, so how does one determine which stories to tell, how many stories will be needed, or how to tell stories in culturally appropriate ways? Spending time in the culture, employing worldview identification instruments, learning the language, and adapting to the culture will enable the missionary to design the story set that will speak to the people. In addition to the basic Bible truths that they need to learn, the missionary must identify the specific issues among them that need to be addressed (issues such as murder, adultery, drunkenness, idolatry, etc.). Bible stories can be selected that will teach the mind of God on these issues as the oral Bible continues to take shape, and that will communicate a biblical worldview.

Some missionaries have developed story sets that can be shared in a matter of hours, while others employ sets that require weeks or months before getting the people to the story of the cross. Such story sets lead hearers to understand the truth and surrender to Jesus Christ as Lord. Although missionaries have primarily used Chronological Bible Storying for evangelism, the usefulness of this tool for discipling, training, and point-in-time teaching continues to grow.

Even among literates, Chronological Bible Storying is a useful tool for developing a biblical worldview. One of my students at the seminary where I teach in the United States had shared the gospel with his mother for over thirteen years and been rejected every time. I suggested that he share the gospel with her using CBS. He met with her weekly for lunch. Each time he told a story and walked through a discovery time with her. When he got to the cross, she did, too. She prayed to receive Christ, was baptized, and joined their church. Her worldview was changed and she finally understood the truth.

CHALLENGES AND SOLUTIONS

Oral theological seminaries have been utilized in places such as the Sudan and India. In these seminaries, there are no computer labs or libraries . . . or even pen, pencil, or paper. All of the instruction is conducted orally. In a typical curriculum, the students will spend the first year learning fifty stories—from creation to the cross—for the purpose of evangelism. In addition to the stories, they may also learn two or more songs that go with each story. The second year of seminary consists of learning fifty more stories and two songs for each that are useful for discipleship. The third year is for learning fifty more stories and two songs for each that will be useful for leadership training and doctrinal instruction. There may be some overlap in the stories, and there will be some narrative-style telling of didactic portions—especially in the upper levels—but the purpose of the story and application is made clear.

In addition to imparting a biblical worldview, the stories of the Bible are useful for point-in-time teaching. For instance, a missionary arriving in a community and finding that a church member is living in sin with a woman could gather the members and tell the story of the man in 1 Corinthians 5. In this way, he would be giving instruction from God's Word and showing very plainly how the situation should be handled. The alternative to this is the missionary declaring that this is wrong and demanding the solution. This may leave the members of the community unsure whether such instruction came from God or the missionary's personal opinion. If the missionary should lose favor in the future, it is possible that all of his "personal opinion" teachings would be set aside as well. The telling of the Bible story, repetition by the hearers to cement it, the application drawn out, and the resolution of the church are all parts of storying the Bible to the hearers.

MY WIFE AND I have been doing "theological education" in India for the last eight years as an in-service training model, using biblical storytelling exclusively. We found that in six four-day modules over a two-year period (plus an exam module) we are able to teach the workers to tell one hundred stories from Genesis through the Gospels. This equates to sixty-five chapters from the Old Testament and eight hundred verses from the New Testament.

Each storyteller is required to train at least one other person to tell all of the stories, and these storytelling disciples are tested on the final exam along with their teachers. Even though the requirement is to teach only one person to tell the stories, in practice most have multiplied themselves many times over. We identified a number of cases where the stories were passed along to four or even five "generations" of tellers and listeners.

—PAUL F. KOEHLER
President, King's Commission Ministries, Inc.

None of this is to imply that primary oral learners cannot hear and understand the words of literate teaching styles. With significant assistance, they may be able to attend a traditional classroom school, obtain the skills necessary to do the work, and score well on tests. However, this does not ensure that they will be able to share this truth with their oral communities. The skill to translate the literacy-based instruction to the oral peoples in their community is not innate, and it is hard work. Two computers that use different operating systems, such as a Mac and a PC, can illustrate this. The hard drive of a Mac can be segmented and the segmented portion dedicated to handle some PC programs and files. In this way, if a PC virus should invade the computer, the entire hard drive will not be infected, only the segmented portion. This compartmentalization also occurs in the minds of oral learners when they develop the skills to perform in literacy-based classes. The part of their brain that they utilize in class is compartmentalized. They may have the information, but it may never find its way into the oral culture. Selected students in oral cultures can learn to read and write reports for literates, but that part of their learning is segmented and dedicated to "school" culture.

The challenges of education and deep discipleship in oral cultures cause many missionaries to shrink from the task and despair of attempting it. How can such cultures be trained? Is it worth the investment of time and human and financial resources to do so? Why not share the gospel in a way that the people can understand, remember, and retell, and then head out for the next group? Do they really need to be trained?

In addition to the challenges of trying to teach oral cultures with oral methods, there is the ever-present threat of error creeping in without the Bible as a static text. The missionary may decide to move on and hope that someone will come in later to translate the Bible and establish a school to teach literacy so that the nationals can be discipled and taught. Sometimes a young national from the oral culture will be selected, taught the skills necessary for learning in the dominant culture's seminary, and funded—from the missionaries' pockets—to attend the seminary. After graduating, the missionaries will try to convince him to return to his community to pastor. They will also need to convince the church members that a young man can be their "elder." Assuming success in all of this, the young man often gives up on his own people as unable to learn—not realizing that he is trying to teach them just as he learned—because they do not have the skills for literacy-based instruction. Sadly, history shows that many missionaries move on at this point. They consider the people reached and abandon their training efforts, believing that the young man they trained ought to be able to train the rest.

CONCLUSION

Oral people must be trained using educational models that are culturally appropriate. The fact is that many oral cultures will never embrace literacy. Even cultures that learn literacy often abandon it and return to orality. Too many Bible translators have said that the happiest day of their ministry was when they gave a completed Bible to the target culture after many years of work; the saddest day was when they returned to visit a few years later and found the Bibles still in boxes. They may have loved their translating missionary, but literacy is just not valued among many cultures.

Educating oral peoples is challenging and depends upon their faithful memories. However, studies continue to show that oral cultures accurately retain more information for longer periods of time than literates. That is because they must remember it; anything forgotten is lost forever since they cannot look back in their notebooks to refresh their memories. The Holy Spirit's role in superintending the transmission of the oral traditions is certainly pertinent here as well. The teachers among them should seek to instill a high value of accuracy in retelling the stories.[12] Certainly, a static text and literate hearers would be better for literate teachers, but you cannot reach and teach people where you wish they were, only where they actually are.

Suggested Reading

Hiebert, Paul G. *Anthropological Insights for Missionaries.* Grand Rapids: Baker Academic, 1986.

Klem, Herbert. *Oral Communication of the Scripture: Insights from African Oral Art.* Pasadena, CA: William Carey Library, 1981.

Nettles, Tom J. *Teaching Truth, Training Hearts: The Story of Catechisms in Baptist Life.* Amityville, NY: Calvary Press, 1998.

Ong, Walter J. *Orality and Literacy.* New York: Routledge, 2002.

Schnabel, Eckhard J. *Paul the Missionary: Realities, Strategies and Methods.* Downers Grove, IL: InterVarsity Press, 2008.

Steffen, Tom A. *Reconnecting God's Story to Ministry: Crosscultural Storytelling at Home and Abroad.* Colorado Springs: Authentic, 2005.

Willis, Avery. *Making Disciples of Oral Learners.* International Orality Network, 2007.

10

CRITICAL CONTEXTUALIZATION: THE BALANCE BETWEEN TOO FAR AND NOT FAR ENOUGH

New missionaries often struggle to communicate God's Word faithfully to other cultures . . . or at least they should. Differences in culture come in many forms. For instance, some cultures have seven primary colors, others recognize only four, and some only have the ideas of shiny and dull. Given these realities, how would you translate Isaiah 1:18, "Come now, let us reason together, says the Lord: though your sins are like scarlet, they shall be as white as snow; though they are red like crimson, they shall become like wool," in a culture that doesn't have scarlet, white, red, snow, or wool? Yet, the Malagasy-speaking peoples' language in Madagascar distinguishes over one hundred colors and recognizes over two hundred kinds of noises. Which word best describes Jesus' journey to Emmaus or His walking on water in the Zulu language, which has 120 words for *walking*? One missionary in the Congo consistently used a phrase for "crying out" to describe John the Baptist or the Old Testament prophets, until one day when he discovered that this referred to the kind of crying that little babies do in their cribs.[1] We must acknowledge that faithfully rendering God's Word in another culture and language is not an easy task.

Preachers and missionaries must continually strive to communicate the gospel so their hearers can understand the message and embrace Christ as their only hope of salvation. Effective gospel communicators take into consideration their cultural context, especially when preaching to the unreached or unchurched. In this chapter we will explore contextualization and its necessary uses and limitations.

RECLAIMING CONTEXTUALIZATION

Some ministers believe that Paul never contextualized the gospel, and so they will not do so either. This belief indicates that they either do not understand the term *contextualization* or that they have redefined it. When anyone dismisses the use of inappropriate vocabulary employed by some preachers, misunderstanding this to be contextualization, they often throw the baby out with the bathwater. Yet, these very detractors contextualize every Sunday. They preach in English, not Greek or Hebrew; they wear suits and ties, not robes or togas; and they employ contemporary illustrations in their sermons, not those from daily life in ancient biblical times. In fact, when the pastor prepares his message for delivery on Sunday morning, he contextualizes the biblical message as he thinks about his audience and the words, mannerisms, and illustrations that will communicate best.

The "children's sermon" is another example of widely accepted contextualization in Western evangelicalism. In many churches before the preaching begins, the pastor invites all the children to come to the front and sit on the steps surrounding the pulpit so he may sit among them to deliver a children's message. He tells them his "sermon" in simplified terms, using a pleasant tone of voice and nonthreatening gestures. A few minutes later, the same basic message might thunder from the pulpit amid flailing arms, perspiration, and pulpit pounding. He may also share the same message with the Friday evening youth group or with the shut-ins at a nursing home on Monday morning, but each time he will employ a different style of delivery and very possibly include different idioms, illustrations, or vocabulary. If we forbid contextualization in missions, perceiving it to be a threat to the gospel, we will be allowing ourselves the luxury of having something that our hearers may never have—a gospel that they can understand. When traveling pastors preach to or teach those with lower levels of academic attainment, they simplify the same sermon that they preached to a more advanced congregation back home. In fact, as they travel, they contextualize daily life in different contexts as they eat local foods, use the national currency, or drive on the opposite side of the road. The threat facing the gospel and the advance of the kingdom today is not the practice of contextualization; it is a misunderstanding of what the word means.

DOES CONTEXTUALIZATION CHANGE THE GOSPEL?

Some people mistakenly believe that contextualization means changing aspects of Christianity to make it look like the culture, but contextualization is simply the process of making the gospel understood. To ensure that our hearers understand the gospel, we must use their language rather than our own, if ours is nonsense to them. However, this does not mean that mimicking the profane vocabulary or lifestyles of the unchurched is an appropriate use of contextualization. The only reason to communicate in this way would be if the local culture communicated so much in this manner that no message would make sense otherwise. Television programs without such inappropriate language would require subtitles for them so people could understand the message. Of course, there is no culture where this is the case. In fact, much of what many call contextualization is simply an effort to be trendy and edgy. It may be effective, it may even attract a hearing among a certain demographic, and it may not be offensive to all hearers, but that is not contextualizing the gospel; that is marketing.

Issues of contextualization are often sensitive across generations within the same culture. For example, at the time I am writing this, it has been common for some pastors in the United States to seek to be trendy or "hip" as a way to reach the post-Christian, often materialistic culture in which they live and minister. Since this becomes their ministry persona, when these brothers are invited to preach in a traditional church or conference where all the other preachers wear coats and ties, they often refuse to "conform" and still insist on wearing T-shirts, jeans, and flip-flops or sneakers. They hope to communicate that they are not "your dad's old preacher" but rather that they are in step with the culture. However, several truths are at work here. While suits and ties are not biblically required, in certain venues they communicate respect for God's people, God's Word, and God's presence. In another cultural context, a guayabera shirt could do the same, or even the casual clothes that some prefer. However, when leaders wear clothing that is out of the ordinary for another's worship context, they communicate the opposite and seem disrespectful. When they utilize in their home ministries what many consider filthy language, they may make a case that it is the most appropriate and effective. However, when they communicate in a national forum—print or preaching—they are no longer in their home context and such language is inappropriate. It should not surprise them that it is offensive, ineffective, and divisive.

ONE GREAT NEED I see in Brazil today is missionaries to assist Brazilian evangelicals, wrestle with current theological and societal trends, and respond with contextual, yet biblical, responses.

—DAVID BLEDSOE

Urban evangelist and church planting trainer,
Brazil

What kind of language and ministry communicates respect for God's Word, recognizes His presence, and honors Him in how we worship? In one culture, suits and ties may be necessary, while in another Hawaiian shirts may communicate the same. Anabaptist brethren see beards as essential for godly men. However, they must make some adjustment when contextualizing the gospel among the many indigenous people who cannot grow facial hair. Some Christian traditions prefer to worship God by singing metrical psalms, but their missionaries must make adjustments or risk communicating that this is the only way to worship God. Wealthy Westerners who dress in their finery for church are dressing in culturally appropriate clothing to honor God's presence. In similar fashion, we noticed when ministering in the Andes that the Quichua ladies who arrived at the church shortly after daybreak would first unbraid their hair, wash it in the stream fed by melting snows, comb it out, and re-braid it before coming in to worship. No one taught them to do this; it was their way of honoring the Lord with their best as they came into His presence.

Paul wrote in Romans 10:13–15 that all who call on the Lord may be saved, and then he went on to ask a series of questions that point out the importance of hearing the gospel for salvation. It is helpful to consider Paul's question, "How shall they hear?" in a discussion of contextualization. It would be pointless to preach the gospel in English to monolingual Swahili speakers. Instead, we must preach the gospel in culturally appropriate ways that are faithful to God's Word. Missionaries working to communicate the gospel in other ethnolinguistic contexts must constantly strive to contextualize the truth of God's Word. Those working with The JESUS Film Project have spent countless hours—and many ministry dollars—correcting and redubbing portions that they discovered they had rendered incorrectly the first time around in many of the languages where they work. In some instances, the word chosen for "prostitute" was the colloquial term that offended some. In other cases, they chose a dialect for the translation that was actually the language of a warring group and therefore the target culture rejected the message. Effective communication of the gospel requires that new missionaries learn the language, dialect, and accent that their hearers will embrace, in addition to merely understanding. Imagine the welcome a missionary with a deep Southern drawl or Cajun Louisiana accent would receive in the shadows of Harvard University when debating the wisdom of creationism over Darwinian evolution. This imagined scenario highlights how something as seemingly insignificant as an accent contributes to the way a messenger is respected and heard. Failing to consider issues of contextualization will most certainly lead to unnecessary stumbling blocks to the gospel.

Does Contextualization Have Limits?

Controversy has often surrounded the issue of contextualization. Years ago, some missionaries argued that we should allow local cultures to determine the content of the gospel for their people and how Christianity should look. The conservative side of missions rightly argued that the Bible speaks to all cultures and is over them—the Bible informs all cultures and is informed by none. No culture may change the gospel or any content of biblical instruction because someone thinks it would be culturally preferable to do so. Yet even so, effective gospel communicators must take into account the target culture as they preach the gospel.

Because most missionaries and preachers want to avoid anything that would alter the gospel message, they shrink back from the hard work of contextualization. However, if one does not contextualize, he is doing just that—changing the gospel. He becomes a modern-day Judaizer. He is in effect telling his hearers that they must become like him to be saved. While we do not want to remove the *skandalon*, the stumbling stone or offense, of the gospel, we do not want to add to the gospel our extrabiblical requirements. I have previously mentioned a humble, illiterate indigenous believer in Peru who feared for her salvation because she had always been taught that literacy was required for church membership. She equated this with salvation and believed that her inability to read would bar her from heaven when she died. Missionaries in the past did not understand that by adding the literacy requirement to church membership, they were inadvertently teaching the people that the Bible required it. Of course, the Bible does not state anywhere that literacy is required for salvation, but the only thing many people knew about the Bible and Christianity is what the missionaries taught. Therefore, when missionaries added the literacy clause to church membership, they were effectively adding it to salvation.

When missionaries—and preachers—seek to contextualize the gospel, they may wonder how far is far enough and how far is too far. Paul gives us those guidelines. He wrote in 1 Corinthians 9:19–23 that he made adjustments in every lawful way so as to relate the gospel to his hearers in ways they could understand. He also gave the parameters in verse 23, "I do it all for the sake of the gospel." The glory of God and reverence for His revelation should guide us in the limits of contextualization so that we never say or do anything that would bring reproach on Him or alter the gospel message. The goal of contextualization is to be culturally relevant and faithful to God's Word.

Cultural relativism is another misunderstood concept that could help us understand the process of contextualization. When secular anthropologists study cultures, they often see them as silos, distinct from others and as a universe unto themselves. For example, with such a mind-set, they say that when people in a given culture kill the second twin at birth, it is not considered murder if the culture does not see it as such. This perspective is often called cultural relativism, since these secular anthropologists believe that no culture can be fairly compared to another. They say it is all relative and there is no supracultural moral law. Obviously, Christians do not embrace such nonsense; there is a God who has clearly communicated what sin is, and His Word is authoritative in every culture—no matter what the local culture may think.

However, in extrabiblical matters—the aspects of life that God does not address with moral import—we have freedom. All things being equal, it is not more or less sinful to live in a house made of wood, bricks, bamboo, or mud. Nor does it matter to God whether we wear leather shoes, tennis shoes, wooden shoes, or no shoes. We can enter other cultures and communicate the gospel in ways that they can readily understand, making the adjustments that are necessary for them to "hear it"—especially regarding extrabiblical matters. Aspects that may be contextualized include things such as language, music style, musical instruments, clothing style, and building materials. Contextualization adjusts for extrabiblical aspects; the message never changes.

Contextualization is not limited to missionaries and preachers spreading the gospel. The term *glocalization* refers to the ways that multinational corporations carry on the same business in many countries but with subtly nuanced changes. McDonald's still sells hamburgers in Malaysia, but the girls behind the counter wear their paper hats on top of their head-coverings and they call their product "beef burgers," not hamburgers, to avoid offending the Muslims who would never eat ham. We don't eat ham on our burgers either, but the culturally offensive name prevents Muslims from getting near enough to find that out. It is the exact same product but clothed in a culturally sensitive form. Contextualization is essential in missions —not simply trendy or stylish—and it does not water down Christ's message.

Much of the criticism of the practice of contextualization actually stems from the ministries and writings of some missionaries who uncritically allowed their hearers to decide what Christianity should teach and look like in the cultures of the world. It seems that some missionaries have held as high a view of the culture as they did of the Bible. The result was that the cultures dictated which parts of the Bible they thought were appropriate for them and how they would practice Christianity. For instance, based on the belief that baptism means "to declare publicly that one is dead to the old way of life and now walking with Christ," some missionaries and cultures argued that the form of baptism is irrelevant. As a result, a young convert would walk to the community fire in public view of all and declare loudly that he had embraced Christ and was denouncing the old ways of ancestor worship, animism, and magic. He would then cut off the amulets, fetishes, and charms that he once believed protected his body and soul, and throw them into the fire. Some missionaries argued that, culturally speaking, baptism had occurred here. Granted, it would be a powerful public testimony, but biblically this would not be baptism. The importance of form and meaning has come into high profile scrutiny where Christian missionaries are working in Muslim areas.

C1–C6 CONTEXTUALIZATION

A highly controversial contextualization scale referred to as C1–C6 measures the degree to which missionaries are contextualizing Christianity in gospel-hostile Muslim contexts. The C1–C6 scale begins with C1, where virtually no contextualization is evident. This end of the continuum refers to a church in a Muslim country that meets in a building that looks just like countless churches in the USA. The worshipers gather on Sunday for Sunday school at 9:45 a.m. and then move to the sanctuary at 11:00 a.m. Families sit together in pews, facing the suit-and-tie-wearing preacher who preaches from a wooden pulpit with a little sign behind him that reports how many were in Sunday school and brought their Bible that day. The evangelical believers in this congregation call themselves Christians. They sit in the soft glow of stained glass and sing hymns out of the same hymnal that the missionaries used back home, accompanied by an organ and piano. This church could have been lifted from the USA's Bible Belt by a *Star Trek* transporter beam and placed in this Muslim city.

C2 is virtually the same experience, but worship and teaching are conducted in the local language. C3 begins to move toward any measurable contextualization by employing cultural forms that are nonreligious. For instance, the style of worship and dress are those that are seen in everyday life. The C3 church includes more believers from a Muslim background because the contextualized church is more attractive and user-friendly to them, whereas C1 and C2 forms are typically places of worship for believers and have little impact on the non-Christian culture.

C4 churches are contextualized to look more Muslim. For instance, the believers among them keep the Ramadan fast, avoid eating pork and drinking alcohol, and use Islamic religious terms. Although Muslims in the culture do not normally see these believers as Muslims, the C4 believers do not refer to themselves as Christians but rather as "followers of Isa Al-Misah," or Jesus the Messiah. C5 contextualization is where the contextualization controversy normally begins, since believers in this church remain socially and legally Muslims. Indeed, they remain so closely identified with Islam that very often they are simply considered theologically deviant Muslims by others in the culture—especially since the C5 believers call themselves "Muslims who follow Isa." C6 is the ultimate extreme of the scale. The C6 end of the continuum consists of virtually secret believers who continue to identify with Islam.

C1–C6 contextualization raises a host of issues. Should Christians use the word *Allah* to refer to the Christian God? Should Christian missionaries and evangelists use the Quran to evangelize Muslims? As I mentioned previously, such efforts at contextualization are fraught with danger and run the risk of heresy and syncretism. While one can tiptoe through an unmarked minefield, finding a way around it is the wiser plan. Yet, when one has been called to live and work in the minefield, he must contextualize the gospel in ways that hearers can understand and in forms that will influence the rest of the culture. He must also contextualize in ways that are faithful to the Scriptures. In many settings, conducting C1 evangelism would result in immediate expulsion—or worse. If expulsion, the culture would be rejecting the gospel without ever hearing it, as they would have rejected the gospel messengers. The C1 end of the scale might allow the missionary to minister without having to do the hard work of contextualization, but this is neither fruitful nor biblical. When Paul was addressing the Areopagus in Acts 17 he did not begin by saying, "You learned philosophers are ignorant of the truth and I am here to educate you." Instead, he began with observations about their religious fervor and demonstrated knowledge of their city and culture. With the hearing he gained, he spoke truth to listening ears.

C1 contextualization is not contextualization at all, nor is it effective in advancing the kingdom. Rather, it is simply a church for expatriates who want a place to worship like the one they left at home. C6 is not contextualization either; it is delaying contextualized church planting until either a critical mass of sufficient numbers is reached, or it is simply declaring that church is not important. Yet, the New Testament teaches that we are to unite with other believers, be baptized, and at times suffer for our identity with Christ. Demanding that believers observe the Lord's Supper with grape juice and bread in a place that has neither one available is not contextualization (as C1 might demand). The other end of the scale might allow the burning of fetishes, charms, and amulets to serve as baptism, but this is not contextualization either. The search for a God-honoring balance is a struggle. Missionaries must be well trained so that they can guide new believers to understand the gospel in culturally sensitive ways that are faithful to God's Word.

CRITICAL CONTEXTUALIZATION

Critical contextualization provides the needed balance. On one hand, failure to contextualize at all imports a foreign religion and adds extrabiblical requirements to salvation. On the other hand, allowing the culture to contextualize with no theological or biblical limits results in syncretism and aberrant expressions of Christianity. Preaching the gospel to people with a pagan worldview may result in confusion. Preaching John 3:16 to a people who worship a tree or stars or ancestors, and who have no biblical understanding of sin, may result in a show of hands at the invitation, but they will not have understood the gospel and their need for Christ.

Many missionaries provide a biblical worldview by teaching the grand narrative of God's revelation through Chronological Bible Storying. Some detractors of contextualization believe that we need only preach the gospel as we do "back home," and this will be sufficient. However, three-point deductive or inductive sermons that work so well in literate societies do not communicate in primary oral cultures.

PAUL PRACTICED CRITICAL contextualization; he taught it through his ministry and wrote of it in his epistles. His first letter to Corinth expressed his practice (9:21–24), while his second letter encapsulated his philosophy. His motif of ambassador (2 Corinthians 5:20) showcases critical contextualization. Ambassadors were respected emissaries sent by a king to represent him before a foreign power. The ambassador did not deviate from the king's message; at the same time he robed that message appropriately in the linguistic and cultural trappings to ensure understanding and acceptance by the host culture. Critical contextualizers do the same. Their message (or resulting work) must be defined by Scripture and shaped by culture. Every gospel presentation or new church happens in a culture and thus must be shaped by that culture; scriptural definition prevents syncretism by safeguarding the integrity of the message.

—STAN MAY

Chairman and Professor of Missions,
Mid-America Baptist Theological Seminary
Former missionary to Zimbabwe

In other areas, such as matriarchal societies, the mother is the most important figure. Women are bosses, serve as community leaders, rule the home, and inherit from their female family members. If the father is even known, he is viewed as a biological necessity but not as an important person in life. When there is an important male figure, it will be the mother's brother. How should we present the gospel here? Without studying to know the culture to contextualize the gospel properly, a sermon on God the Father would leave the hearers with a deficient view of God. In such cases, should we allow the culture to contextualize at will and require that we preach God the Mother? Or should we strike a compromise and preach God the Uncle? Of course, neither of these options would result in a biblical understanding of the gospel. The missionary preacher who has studied the culture must recognize the challenges to the clear presentation of the gospel and teach the people the biblical view of God as Father. While such a practice flies in the face of modern anthropology, it is the biblical approach to properly contextualizing the gospel and Christianity among a people.

A FOURFOLD MODEL

Many missionaries have found needed guidance in the fourfold critical contextualization model that Paul G. Hiebert developed. Hiebert argued that the modern missions movement began with no idea of contextualization. In the early days of the modern missions period, missionaries followed their countries' colonization path around the world and sought to plant churches like the ones they had back home with little regard for or study of local cultures. The result of such ethnocentrism and theological imperialism was a very foreign-looking religion on the surface and profound syncretism within.

When missionaries began to realize the wisdom and value of studying the cultures of the world along with their languages and religions, the age of contextualization really began. However, uncritical contextualization went too far and resulted in biblical distortion. Missionaries elevated the culture so much that the nationals determined the forms, practice, and content of Christianity. They studied each culture without regard to others, which resulted in its having little connection to the worldwide and historical church. Additionally, since they allowed culturally defined categories of sin to continue, a weak view of sin was common.

Hiebert argued for critical contextualization as a corrective measure.[2] In this approach, missionaries should remain faithful to the Scriptures and sensitive to the culture. Biblically literate and theologically educated missionaries are the safeguards in this model. The four steps Hiebert sets forth are cultural exegesis, scriptural exegesis in hermeneutical community, the critical response, and new contextualized practices.

In the exegesis of the culture, the missionary should first seek to understand the culture rather than immediately judge it. In the same way that the beginning step of biblical exegesis is to unpack the passage before beginning to interpret it, so missionaries must study the culture, history, motivations, and worldview in order to understand it. Cultural informants and participant observation are particularly effective in this effort. In missions history, some missionaries forbade the use of drums in tribal groups after learning that the nationals used drums to summon spirits in pagan ceremonies. Years later, the missionaries learned that the people used drums for both musical instruments and for communicating in many ways. They only used one style of drum and a certain rhythm to summon spirits. Outlawing all drums is tantamount to outlawing use of the Internet upon learning that some have used it for sinful purposes. Even more problematic for some missionaries to China was knowing how to respond when observing a new convert offering flowers and incense to pictures of parents and ancestors while appearing to be praying to them. When challenged, the Chinese believer responded that he was simply honoring his parents as the Bible commands us to do. The fact that the missionaries had spoken of leaving flowers at their families' graves complicated this believer's confusion. From an outsider's perspective, the missionary thought the new brother was continuing to worship his ancestors, while the new brother thought he was simply being obedient to both the biblical admonition and cultural expectation.

The next step is to exegete the Scriptures in a hermeneutical community consisting of the theologically educated missionary along with the discipled believers from the culture. These believers bring profound cultural knowledge that would take decades for a missionary to grasp fully, and the trained missionary brings two thousand years of theological and biblical reflection and interpretation to the table. Hiebert referred to this table as the hermeneutical community where nationals and missionaries can study the Bible together. The insights that our national brothers and sisters bring not only give insight into application of the Scriptures in their culture, but they also help missionaries to see truths in the Bible they may have never seen before due to their own cultural biases.

As the hermeneutical community studies the Scriptures to apply them in a particular cultural context, issues will arise that require cultural and biblical knowledge to address adequately. The missionary's home culture likely has a prohibition against polygamy, may scorn alcohol use, and scoffs at the use of natural herbs. But how should the missionary address polygamy in a culture where this has been the practice for dozens of generations, where communities are tied together by marital alliances, where divorce is unknown, and where wives are completely dependent upon their husbands? How should the missionary view the drinking of chicha, a naturally fermented corn-based drink that is an essential part of the culture's traditions? What about chewing betel nut or chewing coca leaves? Indeed, what about the myriad natural herbs in the pharmacological storehouse among the traditional cultures of the world? Are they hallucinogens, or are they stimulants like coffee? Are they allowable, or does their connection to the herbs of animistic traditional religions render them guilty by association? Many cultures, including the USA, have animistic superstitions. Without the assistance of cultural informants, the missionary may never recognize them or their connection to animism; and, when he does, he will need the nationals' assistance to know whether this is sin to be confronted and called to repentance, or if it is a harmless superstitious old wives' tale.

ADDRESSING SIN AND FUNCTIONAL SUBSTITUTES

The missionary who has studied the culture, discipled a group of brothers and sisters to serve with him in the hermeneutical community, and studied the Bible with them will have identified sinful practices or errant beliefs that he may have never seen on his own. When confronted with such practices, rather than authoritatively dictating the needed change, he may simply ask, "What does the Bible say about this?" Together, they will recognize sins in the culture and develop new functional substitutes. Necessary new practices supplied by the community find ready "buy-in" since cultural representatives suggested them.

For instance, in some regions of the Andes, when a new couple marries, they will spend the first year in the home of the groom's parents. During this year, the groom gathers all the building materials they will need for a new home. When he has amassed all that is necessary, the entire community is called together to build the mudwalled, thatch-roofed house. In addition to providing the building materials, the community workers look to him to provide all the alcohol they can consume as a part of this culture complex. These days of building and celebration often result in drunkenness, fights, and worse. A missionary encountering such a practice might immediately forbid the entire practice in an attempt to put an end to the debauchery. The problem is that the people will see a foreign religion that does not understand their people and is forcing its rules upon them. The natural response is to reject the foreigner's religion; after all, how can a person obtain a house if they accept the foreign religion?

An alternative approach would be for the missionary who recognizes the sinful practices associated with the house-raising to study the Bible in the hermeneutical community and point out to them the biblical teaching on drunkenness and fighting. When the culture sees the problem, the Bible forces them to make a critical response. Their response results in a new substitute practice for the traditional one, thus fulfilling the function of the home building but without the drinking and fighting. The hermeneutical community suggests that the practice continue in exactly the same way except that the groom should supply food, soft drinks, and music groups instead of alcohol. In this way, they will build the house and the culture will embrace the new "nonalcoholic" version as a functional substitute.

A truth in all human interaction is "You cannot not communicate." This awkward grammatical construction emphasizes that all our messages are interpreted and assigned meanings by the receiver. Failure to consider the local worldview and culture results in miscommunication. This is easily seen when a missionary asks a Hindu if he wants to be born again or have eternal life. The Hindu believes that he is trapped in an endless cycle of reincarnations and wants to cease his endless rebirths. The Hindu spurns the missionary's invitation, who in turn chalks it up to a hard Hindu heart. In fact, the hearer was interpreting the missionary's message in a culture and worldview that the missionary did not take into account.

When the preacher or missionary does not understand the culture, language, or rules of the game of life in a society, his presentation of the gospel is often offensive for all the wrong reasons. Then, when hearers reject the cultural misfit who does not understand them or their cultural heritage, they also reject the gospel without even knowing it.

HARMONY AND CONTEXTUALIZATION

An East African proverb states, "When two elephants fight, the grass gets hurt." Similarly, there are potential victims at risk when we debate the value and legitimacy of contextualization, and we dare not overlook the danger. One potential victim is the purity of the gospel message. Another potential victim is the unity that Christ called us to maintain. Jesus said that this testimony of unity would proclaim to the world both that the Father sent Him and that He loves us (John 17:23). While some beliefs will necessarily divide us (indeed, he who stands for nothing, falls for anything), we must strive for unity in the essentials. When we divide and succumb to factious infighting, we lose the testimony that the world so desperately needs to see and hear. A final potential victim is the theme of this chapter: the missiological method of critical contextualization. Preachers and missionaries must present the gospel in culturally appropriate ways, or people will never understand the gospel message Christ sent us to proclaim.

As I taught on the exclusivity of the gospel in the Andean community of San Agustín, an elderly brother asked about the souls of his parents and grandparents. He explained that they had believed in Quichua traditional religions and the syncretism of their animism with Catholicism. Although their small village did not have a priest, one would come once a year or so to perform a Mass. He told me that everything they preached was in Latin and that his parents did not even speak Spanish, much less Latin. Then he asked me what happened to his parents when they died. "Where did they go?" I humbly explained that as I understand God's Word, they did not go to heaven if they had not heard the gospel and been born again. He thought for a moment and responded, "I believe that those priests will have a lot to answer for one day." I felt so superior and vindicated, until my drive back to Quito when God brought to my mind how many times I had preached the gospel in ways that made sense to me with little thought as to how well the people understood my message.

I WAS BAKING under some tin roofing in the Amazonian sun along with a few Haitians in a squatters' village outside the capital city of Cayenne in French Guiana. We were singing in Creole without any instruments.

I reached over and grabbed an empty water bottle lying on the ground and threw some pebbles into it. I started shaking it and making some rhythm. The eight or ten people started laughing and singing with more enthusiasm. It was critical contextualization at its best.

We started our Bible study. Most could not read and just listened. They were eager to learn at this point. The white missionary was one of them.

—DAN SHEARD

Senior Pastor, Calvary Missionary Baptist Church

Adjunct Instructor, Lincoln University

Nationals in our target cultures often see Christianity as the foreigner's religion because so many missionaries fail to, or refuse to, contextualize. Missionaries must learn that a gospel that has not been contextualized is no more culturally appropriate than preaching in English to Mandarin speakers. Failure to contextualize makes the missionary a contemporary Judaizer who is unintentionally changing the gospel by unwittingly telling the nationals that they must become like his home culture before Jesus will accept them. Conversely, allowing the culture to contextualize on its own, without any parameters or theological reflection, results in syncretism and violence to the gospel message. The goal of critical contextualization is to preach, teach, translate, and minister in ways that are both faithful to the Word of God and sensitive to the culture. We must contextualize the gospel message so that our hearers can properly understand it, and we must be critical in the process.

CONCLUSION

Critical contextualization provides a culturally relevant understanding of the gospel, while also ensuring checks against syncretism, and it has a high regard for the authority and sufficiency of the Bible. Critical contextualization also recognizes the work of the Holy Spirit in the lives of believers. It humbly respects the illumination that He brings to their understanding of the Bible and its application to their lives. Additionally, critical contextualization incorporates the safeguard of a theologically trained missionary who keeps the contextualization within the bounds of accepted evangelical beliefs and practice. This results in a commonality between the church in the newly won culture and believers around the world.

It would seem to be much easier to teach the world English and then replicate our existing colleges and seminaries in sufficient numbers and locations to equip leaders for churches that look just like our own. However, the peoples of the world will never embrace the foreigners' religion or hear the gospel clearly in a foreign language. The hard work of critical contextualization requires learning languages and the ways that the various cultures of the world use them in each context. Why would you want to do that? Paul answers in 1 Corinthians 13

that love fuels the Christian life. As tedious and painstaking as critical contextualization may be, it is not some Gnostic secret knowledge; it is more about understanding and loving the people, holding
a high view of God's Word, and trusting the Holy Spirit to guide you.
Paradoxically, if you do not have love, even if you master the tongues
of men and angels, it profits you nothing. If you have love but struggle in the necessary process of critical contextualization, you will
communicate it clearly sooner or later, one way or the other (1 Corinthians 13).

Why include a chapter on critical contextualization in a book
focusing on reaching and teaching the cultures of the world? Missionaries must reach the cultures of the world in culturally appropriate ways that are faithful to the Bible. The resulting church must
be sensitive to cultural realities and not be a foreign import if it is to
survive beyond the first generation and remain relevant. However,
the church must also be faithful to God's Word and embrace sound
evangelical theology if it is to please God and have His blessing. Only
a theologically trained missionary can ensure that this process is
faithful to God's Word and evangelical doctrine in the cultures where
he works, and only discipled, trained, and equipped nationals can
assist him in the process of critical contextualization. Trained missionaries must go forth and train trainers who can continue this
process faithfully.

SUGGESTED READING

Hesselgrave, David J. *Communicating Christ Cross-Culturally.* 2nd
   ed. Grand Rapids: Zondervan, 1991.
   _____. *Contextualization: Meanings, Methods, and Models.*
   Pasadena, CA: William Carey Library, 2003.
Hiebert, Paul G. *Transforming Worldviews: An Anthropological
   Understanding of How People Change.* Grand Rapids: Baker
   Academic, 2008.
Piper, John and Justin Taylor, eds. *The Supremacy of Christ in a
   Postmodern World.* Wheaton: Crossway, 2007.

Shaw, R. Daniel and Charles E. Van Engen. *Communicating God's Word in a Complex World*. Lanham, MD: Rowman & Little-field Publishers, 2003.

Van Rheenen, Gailyn. *Communicating Christ in Animistic Contexts*. Pasadena, CA: William Carey Library, 1996.

————, ed. *Contextualization and Syncretism: Navigating Cultural Contexts*. Pasadena, CA: William Carey Library, 2006.

CONCLUSION

Missiology matters. Ideas have consequences. Your philosophy will drive your missiology. Such phrases are more than mere clichés. The truth is, what you think will drive what you do; that is why it is so important to think clearly and believe rightly. Missiologists who are zealous to reach the unreached as fast as possible have devised and implemented strategies and methodologies to speed the work of missions. The motivation driving their efforts is the belief that Jesus provided the formula for facilitating His return. Therefore, they have redefined the task of missions to be that of reaching and leaving as many as possible as fast as possible in order to complete the task. They send and are sent to preach in the unreached areas of the world in order to bring about the second coming of Christ as quickly as possible. But this overwhelming desire keeps them moving on quickly and leaving confusion behind. They justify this by the belief that if they can hasten His return, the untaught will not remain so for long; Jesus will be coming soon.

There is greater awareness and more research data available today than ever before on the topic of the unreached people groups of the world. Moreover, the spotlight is increasingly focused on the groups who are not only UPGs, but where no one is seeking to plant churches. The goal of most contemporary missionary strategies is simply to reach and leave them. However, to be faithful to the command of Christ in the Great Commission, it is crucial that we employ every effort to reach and teach the groups in these places, spreading the gospel and contextualizing it in biblically responsible, culturally appropriate ministry.

Philemoni was nineteen years old with a new wife and new employment as the guard and yard worker for the new American missionary to Mwanza, Tanzania. In 1984 this eager, young African Christian asked to be included in my first TEE (Theological Education by Extension) class, accredited by our mission's national seminary. In halting Swahili, I taught him and a number of other young men a series of courses leading toward a certificate in Bible and Theology.

In order to complement Philemoni's academic training, one Sunday I invited him to go with me on a church planting visit to an outlying neighborhood. We witnessed to a traditional medicine man (some would have called him a witch doctor) who later received Christ as Savior and Lord. Through the witch doctor's influence, Nyakato Baptist Church was started in the neighborhood. Four years later I departed Mwanza, Tanzania to begin our mission board's work in Northern Sudan. I asked Philemoni, with the concurrence of the church, to become the part-time pastor of the still-fledging congregation.

I returned to Mwanza on a mission trip eighteen years later. Years earlier, Philemoni had become the full-time pastor of the self-supporting church. Nyakato Baptist Church had grown to become the second largest Baptist church in Northwestern Tanzania. Philemoni proudly showed me the first TEE book from those early days of discipleship.

Philemoni's tribe, the Sukuma, are a Bantu people. Philemoni told me how he had observed a number of Maasai tribesmen lounging around Mwanza during the daytime, resting from their night watchmen's positions. Philemoni reached out to these men from a non-Bantu background, across tribal and linguistic barriers, witnessing to a dissimilar people group. Remarkably, during a church service where I brought the message, I noticed in the congregation about fifteen men dressed in the traditional red robes of the Maasai mixed in with the Western-style clothing of the Sukuma tribe who make up the majority of Nyakato Baptist Church.

To be honest, I had never suggested to Philemoni that he reach out to a people group beyond his own tribe. I just began the discipleship process and the Holy Spirit led him in paths I could not have imagined.

—ROBIN HADAWAY
Associate professor of missions,
Midwestern Baptist Theological Seminary
Former missionary, Sudan, Tanzania,
and eastern South America

Sadly, missions history shows that in our rush to reach as many UPGs as possible, we may be creating new ones. How is that possible? Consider the 10/40 Window and the regions that we know have the least access to evangelical witness. These regions are now seen as priority areas for needed evangelism, as they reflect the places with the lowest numbers of believers. Yet, remember that some of the greatest centers of Christianity were once in Syria, Egypt, and the regions of Mesopotamia that are now part of the 10/40 Window.

History reveals that once missionaries have planted a church and declared a group reached, there is no guarantee that it will remain so. Likewise, consider Western Europe, which was once the magnificent Christian motherland that sent missionaries to the Americas. Western Europe is now decreasing in its percentage of evangelical Christians at such alarming annual rates that its statistics rival much of the 10/40 Window. Most Europeans view Christianity as irrelevant and passé. All you have to do to create an unreached people group is to abandon a reached one and allow it to return to the old ways.

There are seasons in ministry. Ecclesiastes 3:1–8 teaches that there is a season for everything. I have argued that the biblical balance between searching and harvesting, reaching and teaching, and leaving to search again is not a percentage formula, nor is it a mutually exclusive dichotomy requiring an either/or answer. Instead, the balance between search and harvest strategies is following the leading of the Holy Spirit and being faithful to the commands of God's Word, because both ends of the continuum are valid, biblical, and essential. He knows, He equips, He leads, and He supplies in order that we may do His work. Some pioneer missionaries arrive on the field, see hearers come to Christ, and begin to sense God leading them to shift to a ministry of discipling. This guidance may continue to develop and change as they engage in leadership training or pastoral preparation. One of the essential elements to hearing their missionary call is to get and stay close to the Lord to hear His still, small voice. To know His guidance in daily ministry requires the missionary to stay there.

There is always a struggle for balance in all aspects of ministry. Matters of balance are not as exciting as finding the "tipping point" that leads an entire population to adopt Christianity or being on the cutting edge of innovation in gospel advance. Missionaries and their agencies must resist the temptation to abandon the ministries God gave them to follow what they believe to be more exciting paths. Some missionaries once jokingly shared with me a common saying among them, "He who writes the best report gets the most support." The truth of that statement drives much of the philosophy, methodology, and strategy of contemporary missions. However, missionaries must remain faithful to God's calling and not slip into the paths of least resistance or sail by the changing winds of popular opinion.

Being content to find and maintain the balance that God desires requires patience; and patience is a virtue that is not nurtured in our instant gratification, microwave, and high-speed Internet world. Yet, faithful missionary service that continues to the finish line is pleasing to God and is harder to sustain than a flash in the pan. William Carey, the father of modern missions, claimed that "plodding faithfully" was the key to accomplishing all he did. He said that he could plod and persevere in any pursuit. Likewise, Rachel Saint, who moved into "Auca" territory after the martyrdom of her brother and his four friends, stayed and lived among them, reaching and teaching until her death. "Isn't it something," she asked, "that the Lord Jesus would have used someone like me to do His work in this special place? I was too old by the time I could apply for missionary service. I couldn't help the Waodani much medically, I was not a Bible scholar, and I was never really a superior translator." When her nephew asked why she thought God had given her this assignment and used her in this way, she answered, "Well, Stevie Boy, I loved the Lord Jesus with all my heart, and I trusted Him completely. And I guess I just learned to persevere in whatever He gave me to do."[1]

So many of those who made the greatest difference in missions history were not those who promoted fads or adopted the latest innovations; they simply loved Jesus with all their heart and persevered in what He gave them to do. Being faithful to the task that God gives you to do may put your name in headlines, or you may toil away in anonymity and buried in obscurity the rest of your life, but being faithful is what pleases the Father. And, at the end of the day, that is what you truly want, and that is what you know will make all the difference. There you will find peace because you glorify God in being faithful, patient, and true to His Word, and leaving the results to Him.

The task of international missions today is not just to reach and leave, but rather to reach and disciple and teach the nations. The need for speed tempts us to evangelize and move on. New believers are often the first to see the error of such thinking. Bill Taylor wrote, "The [Latin American nationals] do want [missionaries] to come, but they want them to live with the people, to learn from the people, to love the people, to serve the people, to understand their history, to appreciate their culture, to work alongside and perhaps under them as time develops. They do not speak, as expatriate missionaries tend to do, of 'working yourself out of a job.' It is more, 'Stay with us and work until the task is completed.'"[2] This book has sought to bring awareness to those who have been lulled into the thinking that God wants us to simply reach them. He doesn't. He wants us to reach and teach—reaching them with the saving gospel message and teaching them to observe everything that He has commanded.

ACKNOWLEDGMENTS

Hundreds of people have given input, planted ideas, and influenced this book. Many of them are faithfully serving the Lord as missionaries with a pure desire to advance Christ's kingdom and bring Him glory. Their insights into blessings and dangers in their specific ministry contexts have been poured into the observations and conclusions of this book and make it a much richer and more useful resource than it ever could have been otherwise. Many other insights in this book came from missions professors who are both preparing students for effective intercultural ministry and counseling their graduates already sent out who are encountering the problems enumerated in this book. Indeed, the wisdom, suggestions, and insights of pastors, missionaries, missions professors, mission agency administrators, and church members are sprinkled throughout the pages of this book. Without their insights, this book would have been little more than dry academic theory.

In addition to standing on the shoulders of these giants, God has allowed me to travel the world reaching, preaching, and teaching in Europe, Africa, Asia, South America, Central America, North America, and the Caribbean. The people I have met, churches where I have worshiped, cultures I have experienced, and lessons I have learned are distilled in the pages of this book. As a result, I cannot claim exclusive creative authorship over anything but the mistakes that it contains. I am forever indebted to the missionaries, pastors, church members, students, and professors who have so willingly listened to, added to, and critiqued my thinking along the way. I am also thankful for the insights gained through my association with the Evangelical Missiological Society. The opportunity to present some of this content in the form of academic papers at regional and national society meetings, along with the question and answer interaction, provided polish from the professional missiologists whom I respect so much.

I am very thankful to everyone at Moody Publishers for believing in this project. I appreciate their professionalism, encouragement, and editorial insights. I want to thank specifically Acquisitions Editor Dave DeWit and the Church Life and Reference Team. I am also indebted to Dana Wilkerson and her insights in editing the manuscript to clarify and hone my writing.

My colleagues and students at The Southern Baptist Theological Seminary have been invaluable to me as I researched and reflected upon the missiological, philosophical, and strategic issues pertinent to reaching and teaching the nations. Students who offered their assistance in research were a great encouragement to me during the hard stretches in the midst of a busy academic year. My Garrett Fellow and Ph.D. student, Will Brooks, was a help to me both in researching aspects for the book as well as helping me with my academic load as I wrote.

One of the great helpers during the writing of my first English book, *The Missionary Call*, was Jennifer Lyell. As an editor at Moody Publishers, she went above and beyond the call of duty to polish that work and to make it as successful as it has been. She has spent hours on research for this book as well. She has helped with editing, formatting, fact checking, and emailing back and forth to improve it. She has pushed me to refine my arguments and encouraged me to complete the work when my time was stretched too thin and I was tempted to give up.

I thank my precious family. In addition to allowing me the freedom to dedicate what little time I have to writing, Mary has read every page of the manuscript and made helpful suggestions that have improved its quality. Molly, my little "Daddy's girl," has also been a constant encourager and never complained about the time I spent researching and writing. Christopher and Carol are a constant blessing to me in my life and ministry. Since they are on the cusp of their missionary career, they were much in my mind as I was writing. May God use this book as a tool and resource to bless them and all who read it with effective, God-honoring, and Christ-exalting ministry.

APPENDIX

SOUTHERN BAPTIST
CONVENTION
INTERNATIONAL MISSION
BOARD STATEMENT
ON ECCLESIOLOGY[1]

INTERNATIONAL MISSION BOARD, DEFINITION OF A
CHURCH, JANUARY 25, 2005

The definition of a local church is given in the 2000 edition of the Baptist Faith and Message:

A New Testament church of the Lord Jesus Christ is an autonomous local congregation of baptized believers, associated by covenant in the faith and fellowship of the gospel; observing the two ordinances of Christ, governed by His laws, exercising the gifts, rights, and privileges invested in them by His Word, and seeking to extend the gospel to the ends of the earth.

Each congregation operates under the Lordship of Christ through democratic processes. In such a congregation each member is responsible and accountable to Christ as Lord. Its scriptural officers are pastors and deacons. While both men and women are gifted for service in the church, the office of pastor is limited to men as qualified by Scriptures.

GUIDELINES

We believe that every local church is autonomous under the Lordship of Jesus Christ and the authority of His inerrant Word. This is as true overseas as it is in the United States. Some churches to which we relate overseas may make decisions in doctrine and practice which we would not choose. Nevertheless, we are accountable to God and to Southern Baptists for the foundation that we lay when we plant churches, for the teaching that we give when we train church leaders, and for the criteria that we use when we count churches. In our church planting and teaching ministries, we will seek to lay a foundation of beliefs and practices that are consistent with the Baptist Faith and Message 2000, although local churches overseas may express those beliefs and practices in different ways according to the needs of their cultural settings. Flowing from the definition of a church given above and from the Scriptures from which this definition is derived, we will observe the following guidelines in church planting, leadership training and statistical reporting.

1. A church is intentional about being a church. Members think of themselves as a church. They are committed to one another and to God (associated by covenant) in pursuing all that Scripture requires of a church.

2. A church has an identifiable membership of baptized believers in Jesus Christ.

3. A church practices the baptism of believers only by immersing them in water.[2]

4. A church observes the Lord's Supper on a regular basis.

5. Under the authority of the local church and its leadership, members may be assigned to carry out the ordinances.

6. A church submits to the inerrant Word of God as the ultimate authority for all that it believes and does.

7. A church meets regularly for worship, prayer, the study of God's Word, and fellowship. Members of the church minister to one another's needs, hold each other accountable, and exercise church discipline as needed. Members encourage one another and build each other up in holiness, maturity in Christ, and love.

8. A church embraces its responsibility to fulfill the Great Commission, both locally and globally, from the beginning of its existence as a church.

9. A church is autonomous and self-governing under the Lordship of Jesus Christ and the authority of His Word.

10. A church has identifiable leaders, who are scrutinized and set apart according to the qualifications set forth in Scripture. A church recognizes two biblical offices of church leadership: pastors/elders/overseers and deacons. While both men and women are gifted for service in the church, the office of pastor/elder/overseer is limited to men as qualified by Scripture.

NOTES

Chapter 1: Teaching Them: The Great Omission of the Great Commission

1. So the question arises, "Is our understanding of a people group even correct, i.e., is it God's understanding of a people group (*ethne*)?"

2. World Council of Churches, "Nigerian Baptist Convention," http://www. oikoumene.org/en/member-churches/regions/africa/nigeria/nigerian-baptist-convention.html.

3. C. F. Eaglesfield, *Listen to the Drums* (Nashville: Broadman and Holman Publishers, 1950), 3.

4. Philip Jenkins, *The Next Christendom: The Coming of Global Christianity* (Oxford: Oxford University Press, 2002), 2.

5. Christopher J. H. Wright, *The Mission of God: Unlocking the Bible's Grand Narrative* (Downers Grove, IL: InterVarsity Press, 2006), 38.

6. Harvey Cox, "Christianity Reborn," *The Economist*, December 23, 2006, 49.

7. Paul G. Hiebert has addressed this point repeatedly in his writing through the years, but most specifically with Shaw and Tiénou in *Understanding Folk Religion*. (Hiebert, Shaw, and Tiénou 1999)

Chapter 2: Missionaries Training Nationals: How Much Is Enough?

1. David Garrison, *Church Planting Movements* (Richmond, VA: IMB, 1999), 44.

2. Ibid., 47.

3. James Petigru Boyce, "Three Changes in Theological Institutions," an inaugural address delivered at Furman University, July 31, 1856, http://www.founders. org/library/three.html.

4. David Allen Bledsoe, "A Plea to Reconsider TE Engagement," an unpublished paper, 6.

5. Ralph Winter, "The Editorial of Ralph D. Winter," *Mission Frontiers* 18 (March/April 1996): 1.

6. "Three things are never satisfied; four never say, 'Enough': Sheol, the barren womb, the land never satisfied with water, and the fire that never says, 'Enough.'"

7. W. Harold Fuller, *Mission-Church Dynamics* (Pasadena, CA: William Carey Library, 1980), Appendix G.

Chapter 3: The Bare Minimum: What Must We Teach?

1. Hoyt Lovelace, "Is Church Planting Movement Methodology Viable? An Examination of Selected Controversies Associated with the CPM Strategy," paper presented at the Evangelical Theological Society Spring Southeast Regional Conference, 2006.

2. David Allen Bledsoe, "A Plea to Reconsider TE Engagement," an unpublished paper, 8.

3. Peter Adam, "Preaching and Biblical Theology," in *New Dictionary of Biblical Theology: Exploring the Unity & Diversity of Scripture*, ed. Brian S. Rosner, T. Desmond Alexander, Graeme Goldsworthy, and D. A. Carson (Downers Grove, IL: InterVarsity Press, 2000), 104.

4. James F. Engel, "Beyond the Numbers Game," *Christianity Today,* August 7, 2000, 54.

5. Paul Washer, "Gospel 101," *HeartCry Magazine* 54 (September–November 2007): 6.

6. Donald McGavran, *Ethnic Realities and the Church: Lessons from India* (Pasadena, CA: William Carey Library, 1979), 129.

7. *POUCH Churches*, International Mission Board presentation (2008), slide 21.

8. Washer, "Gospel 101," 1.

Chapter 4: Missionaries and Nationals: Who Should Teach?

1. HeartCry Missionary Society, "Indigenous Missions," http://www. heartcrymissionary.com/ministry/indigenous_missions.

2. Paul Washer, "Indigenous Missions," *HeartCry Magazine* 56 (February 2008): 23.

3. HeartCry Missionary Society, "Comparative Strategies," http://www. heartcrymissionary.com/ministry/indigenous_missions/comparative_strategies.

4. Paul G. Hiebert, R. Daniel Shaw, and Tite Tiéou, *Understanding Folk Religion: A Christian Response to Popular Beliefs and Practices* (Grand Rapids: Baker, 1999), 19–21.

5. Hoyt Lovelace, "Is Church Planting Movement Methodology Viable? An Examination of Selected Controversies Associated with the CPM Strategy," paper presented at the Evangelical Theological Society Spring Southeast Regional Conference, 2006, 39.

6. Donald McGavran, *Ethnic Realities and the Church: Lessons from India* (Pasadena, CA: William Carey Library, 1979), 130.

7. Washer, "Indigenous Missions," 23.

8. David Allen Bledsoe, "A Plea to Reconsider TE Engagement," an unpublished paper, 3.

9. McGavran, *Ethnic Realities and the Church: Lessons from India*, 258.

10. Paul Washer, "The Indigenous Missionary Advantage," *HeartCry Magazine* 56 (February 2008): 18.

11. Judith E. and Sherwood G. Lingenfelter, *Teaching Cross-Culturally: An Incarnational Model for Learning and Teaching* (Grand Rapids: Baker Academic, 2003).

12. James W. Stigler and James Hiebert, *The Teaching Gap* (New York: Simon & Schuster, 1999), 11.

13. Ibid., 87.

14. Ibid., 97.

Chapter 5: Learning from Paul: Missiological Methods of the Apostle to the Gentiles

1. Elisabeth Elliot, *Shadow of the Almighty: The Life & Testament of Jim Elliot* (San Francisco: Harper Collins, 1958), 54.

2. Benjamin L. Merkle, "The Need for Theological Education in Missions: Lessons Learned from the Church's Greatest Missionary," *The Southern Baptist Journal of Theology* 94:4 (Winter 2005): 55.

3. Ibid.

4. Rose Dowsett, *The Great Commission*, Thinking Clearly Series (Grand Rapids: Kregel, 2001), 30.

5. John Polhill, *Paul and His Letters* (Nashville: B&H Publishers, 1999), 442.

6. Paul Barnett, *Paul: Missionary of Jesus* (Cambridge: Eerdmans, 2008), 199.

7. Eckhard J. Schnabel, *Paul the Missionary: Realities, Strategies and Methods* (Downers Grove, IL: InterVarsity Press, 2008), 329–30.

8. Polhill, *Paul and His Letters*, 98.

9. Barnett, *Paul; Missionary of Jesus*, 157.

10. Schnabel, *Paul the Missionary*, 32–33.

11. Roland Allen, *Missionary Methods: St. Paul's or Ours?* (Cambridge: Lutterworth Press, 2006), 17.

12. Schnabel, *Paul the Missionary*, 237–48.

13. Ibid., 237.

14. Merkle, "The Need for Theological Education in Missions," 50.

15. Polhill, *Paul and His Letters*, 99–100.

16. Eckhard J. Schnabel, *Early Christian Mission*, vol. 2 (Downers Grove, IL: Inter-Varsity Press, 2004), 1547.

17. J. Knox Chamblin, *Paul and the Self: Apostolic Teaching for Personal Wholeness* (Grand Rapids: Baker, 1993), 28.

18. Schnabel, *Early Christian Mission*, 1299.

19. Merkle, "The Need for Theological Training in Missions," 59.

20. Ibid., 59–60.

Chapter 6: Search Versus Harvest Theology: Reaching or Teaching?

1. Patrick Johnstone, email interview, December 30, 2008.

2. Patrick Johnstone, "Covering the Globe," in *Perspectives on the World Christian Movement*, ed. Ralph D. Winter (Pasadena, CA: William Carey Library, 1999), 544.

3. Johnstone, interview.

4. Joshua Project, "Definitions," http://www.joshuaproject.net/definitions.php.

5. Greg Parsons, phone interview, January 15, 2009.

6. Dan Scribner, "Joshua Project Step 1: Identifying the Peoples Where Church Planting Is Most Needed," *Mission Frontiers* 17 (November/December 1995), as accessed at http://www.missionfrontiers.org/pdf/1995/1112/nd955.htm.

7. Todd Johnson, phone interview, December 30, 2008.

8. Ibid.

9. Ibid.

10. Luis Bush, "What Is Joshua Project 2000?" *Mission Frontiers* 17 (November/December 1995), as accessed at http://www.missionfrontiers.org/pdf/1995/1112/nd953.htm.

11. Jarod Cronk, "Joshua Project Step 6: Planting Churches in Each of These Peoples," *Mission Frontiers* 17 (November/December 1995), as accessed at http://www.missionfrontiers.org/pdf/1995/1112/nd9511.htm.

12. James F. Engel, "Beyond the Numbers Game," *Christianity Today,* August 7, 2000, 55.

13. Ibid.

14. Donald McGavran, *Understanding Church Growth*, 3rd ed., ed. C. Peter Wagner (Grand Rapids: Eerdmans, 1990), 192.

15. Alan Walker, *A Ringing Call to Mission* (New York: Abingdon Press, 1966), 31.

16. McGavran, *Understanding Church Growth*, 180.

17. Ibid., 30.

18. Ibid., 39.

19. Ibid., 163.

20. Ibid., 24.

21. Ibid., 26.

22. Mission Frontiers, "The Southern Baptists Restructure to Reach the Unreached Peoples: An Interview with Jerry Rankin, IMB President and Avery Willis, Senior Vice President for Overseas Operations," *Mission Frontiers* 19 (July/October 1997), as accessed at http://www.missionfrontiers.org/pdf/1997/0710/jo976. htm.

23. Eckhard J. Schnabel, *Early Christian Mission*, vol. 2 (Downers Grove, IL: InterVarsity Press, 2004), 1299–1300.

24. Schnabel, *Paul the Missionary: Realities, Strategies and Methods* (Downers Grove, IL: InterVarsity Press, 2008), 287.

25. Bush, "What is Joshua Project 2000?"

26. R. C. Sproul, *Tabletalk*, April 2009, 50.

27. I am not arguing here the merits of the partial preterist position over the dispensational premillennenialist view of such passages, but rather pointing out that warm-hearted evangelical Bible scholars disagree on how they should be interpreted. Such disagreement should warn against either dogmatic adherance or basing our missiology and methodology on a minority opinion.

28. Ralph D. Winter and Bruce A. Koch, "Finishing the Task: The Unreached Peoples Challenge," *Mission Frontiers* (June 2000): 30.

29. Joshua Project, "How Many People Groups Are There?" http://www.joshuaproject. net/how-many-people-groups.php.

30. International Mission Board, "Global Research," http://www.imb.org/ globalresearch.

31. Joshua Project, "Global Summary," http://www.joshuaproject.net.

Chapter 7: Techniques and Tools: The Greater Good, CPMs, and What Only God Can Do

1. Phil Parshall, "Danger! New Directions in Contextualization," *Evangelical Missions Quarterly* 34:4 (October 1998): 404–17.

2. *Webster's Online Dictionary*, s.v. "Charlatan," http://www.websters-online-dictionary.org/definition/charlatan.

3. Tim and Rebecca Lewis, "Planting Churches: Learning the Hard Way," *Mission Frontiers* 31 (January/February 2009): 18.

4. David Garrison, *Church Planting Movements* (Midlothian, VA: WiGTake Resources, 2004), 21.

5. Ibid., 244–45.

6. Avant Ministries, "What Is Short-Cycle Church Planting?" http://www. avantministries.org/what-is-short-cycle-church-planting-2.

7. Hoyt Lovelace, "Is Church Planting Movement Methodology Viable? An Examination of Selected Controversies Associated with the CPM Strategy," paper presented at the Evangelical Theological Society Spring Southeast Regional Conference, 2006, 20.

8. Lovelace, 9–10.

9. Charles Grandison Finney, *Lectures on Revivals of Religion* (Leavitt, Lord & Co., 1835), 25–32.

10. Ibid., 29.

11. Ibid., 32.

12. Ibid.

13. C. C. Goen, ed., "The Morphology of Conversion," in the editor's introduction to *The Great Awakening*, by Jonathan Edwards, as found at The Jonathan Edwards Center at Yale University, http://edwards.yale.edu/archive.

14. J. Gerald Harris, "Shining the Spotlight on the IMB's Church Planting Movement," *The Christian Index*, May 24, 2007, 1.

15. Ibid., 3.

16. Clyde Meador, "The Left Side of the Graph," *Journal of Evangelism and Missions* 6 (Spring 2007): 59–60.

17. Ibid., 4.

18. Ibid., 5–6.

19. Ralph Winter, "Two Responses," *Occasional Bulletin of the Evangelical Missiological Society* 22:1 (Winter 2009): 8.

Chapter 8: Equipping Disciples: Theological Education and the Missionary Task

1. Africa Inland Mission On-Field Media. *Moffat Bible College*, video from AIM International Online, MPEG, http://www.aimint.org/usa/videos/moffat_bible_college.html (accessed September 20, 2009).

2. Eckhard J. Schnabel, *Paul the Missionary: Realities, Strategies and Methods* (Downers Grove, IL: InterVarsity Press, 2008), 248.

3. Greg Wills, "Southern Seminary, Southern Baptists, and the Two Religions" (The Southern Baptist Theological Seminary, March 11, 2009).

4. Africa Inland Mission On-Field Media. *So We Do Not Lose Heart*, video from AIM International Online, MPEG, http://www.aimint.org/usa/videos/so_we_do_not_lose_heart.html (accessed September 20, 2009).

5. Ibid.

6. Merkle, "The Need for Theological Education in Missions," *The Southern Baptist Journal of Theology* 94:4 (Winter 2005): 59.

7. David Claydon, ed. "A New Vision, A New Heart, A Renewed Call," in *Lausanne Occasional Papers from the 2004 Forum for World Evangelization* (Pasadena, CA: William Carey Library, 2006), 9.

8. Africa Inland Mission On-Field Media, *So We Do Not Lose Heart.*

9. John Stam, "The Need for Biblical Teaching in Latin America," Latin America Mission Online, http://www.lam.org/news/article.php?id=410.

10. David Allen Bledsoe, "A Plea to Reconsider TE Engagement," an unpublished paper, 4–6.

11. Mark Dever and Sinclair Ferguson, *The Westminster Directory of Public Worship* (Hagerstown, MD: Christian Heritage, 2008), 3.

12. Ibid., 9.

13. Ibid., 10–11.

14. Bledsoe, "A Plea to Reconsider TE Engagement," 6–8.

Chapter 9: Primary Oral Learners: How Shall They Hear?

1. Actually, people seldom learn anything while they themselves are speaking, but the terms "oral" and "orality" have become standard in modern missiology. Primary "aural" learners would be more technically accurate—meaning that they learn by hearing, not the written word.

2. Durk Meijer, "How Shall They Hear," presentation at International Orality Network Meeting, February 2008.

3. Charles H. Kraft, *Communication Theory for Christian Witness* (Maryknoll, NY: Orbis Books, 1991), 161.

4. Paul G. Hiebert, *Anthropological Insights for Missionaries* (Grand Rapids: Baker Academic, 1986), 45.

5. Paul G. Hiebert defined culture as "the more or less integrated systems of ideas, feelings, and values and their associated patterns of behavior and products shared by a group of people who organize and regulate what they think, feel, and do" (*Anthropological Insights for Missionaries*, 30).

6. Herbert Klem, *Oral Communication of the Scripture* (Pasadena, CA: William Carey Library, 1981), ix.

7. Orality Issues Group, "Making Disciples of Oral Learners," a paper developed at the Lausanne Committee for World Evangelization, Pattaya, Thailand, October 5, 2004.

8. Klem, *Oral Communication of the Scripture,* xvii.

9. Unless otherwise noted, statistics within this chapter are representative of the work completed by the International Orality Network. The most comprehensive expression of this evaluation is found in the *Lausanne Occasional Paper 54,* "Making Disciples of Oral Learners," 2004.

10. Meijer, presentation.

11. Tom J. Nettles, *Teaching Truth, Training Hearts: The Study of Catechisms in Baptist Life* (Amityville, NY: Calvary Press, 1998), 135.

12. Missionary LaNette Thompson draws a chalk circle on the floor when training Bible storyers. When they retell the story, they must step out of the circle if they make a mistake. This teaches them the value of accuracy.

Chapter 10: Critical Contextualization: The Balance Between Too Far and Not Far Enough

1. Eugene Nida, *God's Word in Man's Language* (New York: Harper, 1952), 16.
2. Paul Hiebert, *Anthropological Reflections on Missiological Issues* (Grand Rapids: Baker Books, 1994), 75–92.

Conclusion

1. Steve Saint, *End of the Spear* (Carol Stream, IL: SaltRiver, 2005), 184.
2. William David Taylor, *Crisis and Hope in Latin America: An Evangelical Perspective* (Pasadena, CA: William Carey Library, 1996), 498.

Appendix: Southern Baptist Convention International Mission Board Statement on Ecclesiology

1. This statement is available on the website of the International Mission Board, and at the time of writing is found at http://www.imb.org/main/news/details. asp?LanguageID = 1709&StoryID = 3838#.]
2. Note that this statement is not meant to imply Institute endorsement of a particular form of baptism.

BIBLIOGRAPHY

Adam, Peter. "Preaching and Biblical Theology." In *New Dictionary of Biblical Theology: Exploring the Unity & Diversity of Scripture*, edited by Brian S. Rosner, T. Desmond Alexander, Graeme Goldsworthy, and D. A. Carson, 104–112. Downers Grove, IL: InterVarsity Press, 2000.

Allen, Roland. *Missionary Methods: St. Paul's or Ours?* Cambridge: Lutterworth Press, 2006.

Barnett, Paul. *Paul: Missionary of Jesus.* Vols. 1–2. Grand Rapids: Eerdmans, 2008.

Bush, Luis. "What Is Joshua Project 2000?" *Mission Frontiers* 17 (November/December 1995).

Chamblin, J. Knox. *Paul and the Self: Apostolic Teaching for Personal Wholeness.* Grand Rapids: Baker, 1993.

Claydon, David, ed. "A New Vision, A New Heart, A Renewed Call."
In *Lausanne Occasional Papers from the 2004 Forum for World
Evangelization*. Pasadena, CA: William Carey Library, 2006.

Cox, Harvey. "Christianity Reborn." *The Economist*, December 23, 2006,
48–50.

Cronk, Jarod. "Joshua Project Step 6: Planting Churches in Each of
These Peoples." *Mission Frontiers* 17 (November/December 1995).

Dever, Mark and Sinclair Ferguson. *The Westminster Directory of
Public Worship*. Hagerstown, MD: Christian Heritage, 2008.

Dowsett, Rose. *The Great Commission*. Thinking Clearly Series.
Grand Rapids: Kregel, 2001.

Driscoll, Mark. "The Church and The Supremacy of Christ in a Post-
modern World." In *The Supremacy of Christ in a Postmodern
World*, eds. John Piper and Justin Taylor, 125–48. Wheaton:
Crossway, 2007.

Eaglesfield, C. F. *Listen to the Drums*. Nashville: Broadman and
Holman Publishers, 1950.

Elliot, Elisabeth. *Shadow of the Almighty: The Life and Testament of
Jim Elliot*. San Francisco: Harper Collins, 1958.

Engel, James F. "Beyond the Numbers Game." *Christianity Today*,
August 7, 2000: 54–57.

Finney, Charles Grandison. *Lectures on Revivals of Religion*. New
York: Leavitt, Lord & Co., 1835.

Fuller, W. Harold. *Mission-Church Dynamics*. Pasadena, CA: William
Carey Library, 1980.

Garrison, David. *Church Planting Movements*. Richmond, VA: IMB,
1999.

_____. *Church Planting Movements*. Midlothian, VA: WiGTake
Resources, 2004.

Goen, C. C. ed. "The Morphology of Conversion." In the editor's
introduction to *The Great Awakening*, by Jonathan Edwards, as
found at The Jonathan Edwards Center at Yale University,
http://edwards.yale.edu/archive.

Hiebert, Paul G. *Anthropological Insights for Missionaries.* Grand Rapids: Baker Academic, 1986.

————. *Anthropological Reflections on Missiological Issues.* Grand Rapids: Baker Books, 1994.

Hiebert, Paul G., R. Daniel Shaw, and Tite Tiénou. *Understanding Folk Religion: A Christian Response to Popular Beliefs and Practices.* Grand Rapids: Baker Books, 1999.

Jenkins, Philip. "Covering the Globe." In *Perspectives on the World Christian Movement*, edited by Ralph D. Winter, 541–52. Pasadena, CA: William Carey Library, 1999.

————. *The Next Christendom: The Coming of Global Christianity.* Oxford: Oxford University Press, 2002.

Klem, Herbert. *Oral Communication of the Scripture.* Pasadena, CA: William Carey Library, 1981.

Kraft, Charles H. *Communication Theory for Christian Witness.* Maryknoll, NY: Orbis Books, 1991.

Lewis, Tim and Rebecca Lewis. "Planting Churches: Learning the Hard Way." *Mission Frontiers* 31 (January/February 2009).

Lingenfelter, Judith E. and Sherwood G. Lingenfelter. *Teaching Cross-Culturally: An Incarnational Model for Learning and Teaching.* Grand Rapids: Baker Academic, 2003.

Lovelace, Hoyt. "Is Church Planting Movement Methodology Viable? An Examination of Selected Controversies Associated with the CPM Strategy." Presented at the Evangelical Theological Society Spring Southeast Regional Conference, 2006.

McGavran, Donald. *Ethnic Realities and the Church: Lessons from India.* Pasadena, CA: William Carey Library, 1979.

————. *Understanding Church Growth.* 3rd ed. Edited by C. Peter Wagner. Grand Rapids: Eerdmans, 1990.

Meador, Clyde. "The Left Side of the Graph." *Journal of Evangelism and Missions* 6 (Spring 2007): 59–63.

Merkle, Benjamin L. "The Need for Theological Education in Missions: Lessons Learned from the Church's Greatest Missionary." *The Southern Baptist Journal of Theology* 94:4 (Winter 2005): 50–61.

Mission Frontiers Staff. "The Southern Baptists Restructure to Reach the Unreached Peoples: An Interview with Jerry Rankin, IMB President and Avery Willis, Senior Vice President for Overseas Operations." *Mission Frontiers* 19 (July/October 1997).

Nettles, Tom J. *Teaching Truth, Training Hearts: The Study of Catechisms in Baptist Life.* Amityville, NY: Calvary Press, 1998.

Nida, Eugene. *God's Word in Man's Language.* New York: Harper, 1952.

Orality Issues Group. "Making Disciples of Oral Learners." Developed at the Lausanne Committee for World Evangelization, Pattaya, Thailand, October 5, 2004.

Parshall, Phil. "Danger! New Directions in Contextualization." *Evangelical Missions Quarterly* 34:4 (October 1998): 404–17.

Piper, John, and Justin Taylor, eds. *The Supremacy of Christ in a Postmodern World.* Wheaton: Crossway, 2007.

Polhill, John. *Paul and His Letters.* Nashville: B&H Publishers, 1999.

Saint, Steve. *End of the Spear.* Carol Stream, IL: SaltRiver, 2005.

Schnabel, Eckhard J. *Early Christian Mission.* Volumes 1–2. Downers Grove, IL: InterVarsity Press, 2004.

_____. *Paul the Missionary: Realities, Strategies and Methods.* Downers Grove, IL: InterVarsity Press, 2008.

Scribner, Dan. "Joshua Project Step 1: Identifying the Peoples Where Church Planting Is Most Needed." *Mission Frontiers* 17 (November/December 1995).

Stigler, James W. and James Hiebert. *The Teaching Gap.* New York: Simon & Schuster, 1999.

Taylor, William David. *Crisis and Hope in Latin America: An Evangelical Perspective.* Pasadena, CA: William Carey Library, 1996.

Tippett, A. R. "1970 Retrospect and Prospect." In *Church Growth Bulletin* 6:4 (March 1970): 49–53.

Wagner, C. Peter. "On the Cutting Edge." In *Perspectives on the World Christian Movement*, edited by Ralph D. Winter, 531–40. Pasadena, CA: William Carey Library, 1999.

Walker, Alan. *A Ringing Call to Mission.* New York: Abingdon Press, 1966.

Washer, Paul. "Gospel 101." In *HeartCry* Magazine 54 (September–November 2007): 1–6.

_____. "Indigenous Missions." In *HeartCry* Magazine 56 (February 2008): 16–23.

Wingate, Andrew. "Overview of the History of the Debate About Theological Education." In *International Review of Mission* 94:373 (April 2005): 235–47.

Winter, Ralph. "The Editorial of Ralph D. Winter." In *Mission Frontiers* 18 (March/April 1996).

_____. "Two Responses." In *Occasional Bulletin of the Evangelical Missiological Society* 22:1 (Winter 2009): 6–8.

Wright, Christopher J. H. *The Mission of God: Unlocking the Bible's Grand Narrative.* Downers Grove, IL: InterVarsity Press, 2006.

SUBJECT INDEX

THE MISSIONARY CALL

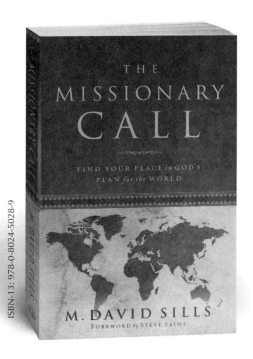

ISBN-13: 978-0-8024-5028-9

Christians of all ages recognize the heartbeat of God to take the gospel to the nations and wrestle with the implications of the Great Commission in their own lives. *The Missionary Call* explores the biblical, historical, and practical aspects of discerning and fulfilling God's call to serve as a missionary. Pointing the reader to Scripture, lessons from missionary heroes, and his own practical and academic experience, Dr. Sills guides the reader to discern the personal applications of the missionary call.

MOODY
PUBLISHERS
MOODYPUBLISHERS.COM

WHEN HELPING HURTS

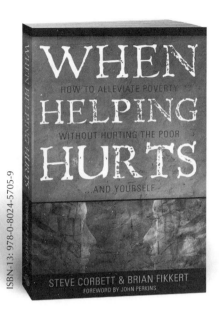

Churches and individual Christians typically have faulty assumptions about the causes of poverty, resulting in the use of strategies that do considerable harm to poor people and themselves. *When Helping Hurts* provides foundational concepts, clearly articulated general principles, and relevant applications. The result is an effective and holistic ministry to the poor, not a truncated gospel.

A situation is assessed for whether relief, rehabilitation, or development is the best response to a situation. Efforts are characterized by an "asset-based" approach rather than a "needs-based" approach. Short term mission efforts are addressed and microenterprise development (MED) is explored.

MOODY
PUBLISHERS

MOODYPUBLISHERS.COM